YOUR STORY STARTS HERE

THE ART OF WRITING, PUBLISHING AND MARKETING YOUR NON-FICTION BOOK

ABIGAIL HORNE

DEDICATION

To my mum,

For being that parent who always made time to read to me as a child: Enid Blyton will always be a favourite because of you.

Thank you for never saying no to buying me a book, even when life was at its hardest.

You have been my strength and biggest supporter my entire life and I thank you with all my heart for everything you have ever done for me and encouraged me to achieve.

Your belief in me is why I believe in myself, and that is the greatest gift you could possibly have given to me as your daughter.

Thank you for simply everything.

(Written during the 2020 Coronavirus Pandemic, while social

distancing has kept us from having a hug but not from having a family walk two metres apart.)

CONTENTS

INTRODUCTION

THE STORY BEHIND THE STORIES

The genetic specialist turned her screen to face me, showing me the cancers within my family tree. The only thing running through my mind was, "Your diagram is soul destroying."

There it was, a box containing my grandad's name with a big red cross going all the way through it.

Edward Hand - Deceased, Non-Hodgkin's Lymphoma.

How was this his legacy? Ok, so I knew him, but in years to come is that all that my children's children are going to know about this incredible man?

My heart just sank, remembering the conversation I had with my grandad during his illness.

"I've bought you a gift, Grand. I think we should fill it in together."

I proudly handed him a sort of journal called, "Dear Grandad, From You To Me". You go through and write on each page, answering the prompts, which eventually fills the book with the author's life story, their memories, knowledge, thoughts and wisdom, in their own words.

I just wanted to cherish it forever, not knowing what was around the corner.

He smiled and said, "I will write in this, but not now... I'm not going anywhere just yet."

I understood, and "not now" continued into his remission. He was given the all-clear and life was back to normal.

The urgency had gone, the anxiety had passed, and the book was put in a drawer.

Twelve months later, with no warning, my grandad's cancer

returned in his brain. Within three weeks I lost my hero and my world fell apart.

How would I continue to face every day of my life without him?

What would his advice for me be on getting married and having children of my own?

What would he think of my career choices?

What would he tell me to do when things get tough?

I don't even know. Because he isn't here to ask… and he never got the book back out of the drawer. Blank page after blank page.

It haunts me.

I survived. This year marks ten years since his passing and life has been filled with happiness and love.

A year after he passed away, I gave birth to a beautiful baby boy, lovingly named after my grandad, Ted. He asks about him all the time and I will forever share my stories and my memories of him… but it's not the same.

I wish I could hand him my grandad's book to be passed down through the generations so his memory would stay alive and intact forever.

Those pages would have kept him immortal, his words and wisdom in written form to cherish, always.

Instead, here I am in a genetic counselling session staring at his name, crossed out. Deceased.

That genetic appointment took place in October 2017. Eight weeks later, I launched Authors & Co with a heart filled with the desire that our legacy be far greater than any diagram.

Sharing our lives' greatest moments, deepest thoughts and wisest teachings is not reserved for celebrities, it is for all of us.

Publishing a book is not reserved for those who have their "Submission Accepted" by printing/publishing houses, it is for ALL of us.

Leaving our greatest legacy in book form is for each and every one of us, no exception.

For too long we have gifted our personal power to an industry worth billions and let them have the final say on whether our story is worth printing. How tragic.

Take back your power, do what my grandad never got around to doing and leave a lasting written legacy within our world.

Now... not never.

Your past experiences may one day change someone's life.

Abigail x

1

THAT DREAM IN YOUR HEART… IS ALSO IN YOUR HANDS

MY PROMISE TO YOU

*M*y purpose in this book is to pass on a wealth of knowledge and experience to help you write your own non-fiction book over the next few months. That's months, not years. I want to give you not only practical guidance, but also the confidence to actually get started.

I am about to share with you a break down some of the key points that I will be addressing throughout the chapters.

(In sharing this with you, I'm helping you make a decision early on as to whether you want to continue reading. Time is so precious, and I only want to take up some of yours if you are committed to writing and publishing your dream book.)

My one big promise to you is that if you stay with me, read this thoroughly and action accordingly, within a few short months of your starting point you will have a manuscript ready to transform into a book.

I'd like you to start by getting into a comfortable sitting position. Place your feet flat on the ground, place your palms facing upwards over your knees and take three deep breaths, inhaling and exhaling slowly.

I want you to visualise what your book looks like in your mind.

- How do you feel opening the brown paper package containing the first copy ever to be printed?
- What does it feel like in your fingertips?
- How does the scent of those brand-new pages make you feel?
- How do you imagine your book launch?
- What does it look like, sound like and taste like?
- What is the aroma you can smell?
- What can you hear around you?
- What are you wearing?
- Who is celebrating with you?
- How do you feel?
- Allow yourself to look even further into the future. How has your life changed?
- How have the lives of others changed?
- Was it all worth it?

I want to support you in making that vision your reality, as

I have done for hundreds of others just like you. Write down all the thoughts and feelings that came into your mind and keep them close as we embark on a journey together to make them your reality.

At this stage I want you to consider, what is your one big promise to your readers? Consider what you are promising the book will deliver to your readers, then follow my lead on breaking it down. This is to help your ideal reader feel confident that it is worth sticking around with you, because they are holding in their hands the answers to what they are looking for.

The breakdown:

First of all, we are going to delve into why I want you to conquer this book writing battle, and to look at the consequences of you ignoring the opportunity that you have your hands on. (Quite literally!)

Then, we will take a look at what I believe to be your biggest obstacles which are holding you back. This isn't guesswork. My findings come from intensive market research collected, compiled and reviewed before starting to write this book.

We will then move on to some facts about self-publishing vs traditional publishing, so that right from the start of this process you have in your mind what option best serves your purpose. There are common misconceptions about both, and I would like to clear those up for you.

After that, we will take a look at some of the pitfalls you may encounter during the book writing process, and of course, how to overcome them.

We will spend a lot of time on how to create the main body of your book. I will be discussing step by step how and what to do. Specifically, this will cover:

- Tangible Outcome – Do you want to generate leads? Reach and inspire a wider audience? Make a direct sale? Raise your profile? Establish yourself as an expert?
- Your Dream Reader – You will have to answer lots of questions to really be sure that your book hits all the right sweet spots!
- Building Your Audience – So that you have loyal fans ready and waiting to support you in getting your book out into the world.
- Creating a Book Blueprint – Your book blueprint is not only the skeleton of your book, but a fabulous reminder of what meat you intend to put on the bones. It can be designed in such a way that every time you sit down to write, you know EXACTLY what you will be writing about, with a word count guideline to keep you on track.
- Writing Habits - Writers are infamous procrastinators. But you don't have to be if you create a writing habit. Throughout this book I will also be demonstrating my own writing habits!

- Writer's Block – I want to uncover some of the most powerful hacks to beat writer's block, forever giving you space and confidence to overcome any writing blocks you may encounter along the way.
- Creating Your First Draft – A major cause of writer's block is trying to make everything perfect in the first draft. I will be explaining what to do and what not to do.
- Beta Readers – A Beta Reader is someone who evaluates a manuscript.
- It's an especially valuable step if you are planning to self-publish, but can also help you in the quest to get an agent or publisher if you are planning on taking the traditional route with your book.
- Editing and Revisions – Again, this section will ask you a series of questions to make you consider a new perspective.
- Your Final Manuscript – The steps to make sure that your book is as good as you can make it as you work on your final manuscript.
- Designing Your Book Cover – How to consider this step as a reader, not a writer.
- ISBNs – What are they and what options do you have?
- Titles, Subtitles & Keywords – What to do, and why!
- Your Book Description – After the title and the cover, the most important marketing material for

your book is the description. We are going to look at getting this bit right!

- A WOW Amazon Author Profile – Why you need one and how it will help you with your goals.

After the writing, we will move on to the bit that most authors like to ignore, the 70% of what it takes to make your book successful.

- Your book marketing plan – Because a step by step plan will help you understand what to do and when to do it.
- A book launch team – Who does it involve and why do you need one?
- Email marketing – What do you need to do and why is it so important?
- A book trailer – Why you need one and what structure you need to follow.
- Podcasts – Why they are amazing for book sales and how to get yourself on them!
- Reviews – Why you need them and how to get them.

At the end of the book, we will look at some kind words, and some of the outcomes of the authors that I have directly worked with.

Finally, if you haven't completely had enough of me by that

point, I will talk you through how we can hang out together more, and how I can continue to support you as an author.

I know that at this point your book still seems an up-hill struggle. We will tackle that by getting focused on the consequences of you not continuing with this process and missing out on one of the best marketing materials that you will ever have your hands on!

THE TRULY EMPOWERED WOMAN

> "Stop looking outside for scraps of pleasure or fulfilment, for validation, security, or love – you have a treasure within that is infinitely greater than anything the world can offer."
>
> — ECKHART TOLLE

This quote was shared by someone this morning. Moments later she followed it up with yet another disappointed update that she has now had her non-fiction book concept rejected by publishers for the twenty-seventh time. This has been going on for three years now, whilst sharing posts to empower others. I have often wondered why this confident and incredible woman has continued to allow herself to be disempowered.

Hundreds of thousands of books get rejected by traditional

publishers every single year. It is a fact that only a very small percentage will ever get accepted. What you need to take away from this is that just because you may be high risk to a publisher, it doesn't mean that your message shouldn't be shared. If you truly have a powerful story or words of wisdom that could take readers through a transformation, you are doing not only yourself, but others a disservice.

As a writer, your default setting when facing any sort of rejection is, "My book proposal isn't good enough, therefore I am not good enough." Before we allow those feelings to consume you, let's take a look at some of the more likely reasons you are now contemplating a new path to publish your work.

You have thought about the outline, but not the position.

Traditional publishers are making an investment in your book when they offer you a contract. This means that beyond the gold you are about to spin between the covers, what they are interested in is whether you are able to convince them as publishers, not marketers, that you have really thought about the positioning of your book within the market place. This is vital to ensure that it sells. If you cannot convince a publisher that you are oozing with market appeal, you are too high risk.

Followers count.

Publishers make their money by taking the lion's share of

book sales, so on weighing up whether their investment is going to pay dividends, they need to see how many potential sales are waiting in the wings. An average of five percent of your following will purchase your book, so unless that figure excites them, again, you are too high risk.

Can I tell you what the saddest part is? It's that if your follower number translated into a cash figure DOES excite them, it means that you don't need them whatsoever. More on that shortly.

A betting game.

Publishers can only work with so many authors. There are only so many hours in the day and team members to work on your project. By saying yes to you, they are saying no to someone else, someone who may be their next Rachel Hollis. They are simply hedging their bets as strategically as possible to try and secure the biggest win.

You see, it's nothing to do with your book not being good enough. That's what editors are for. Manuscripts can be transformed.

Losing confidence.

Many authors wait months and even years to hear back after sending in submissions. As time ticks by, confidence in their writing diminishes, morale is knocked, and eventually they get a 'thanks but no thanks' reply anyway.

The big mistake so many authors make here is to lose their

confidence in themselves, when really, it's nothing to do with them. This can often rob the book industry of some of our greatest potential writers. It's really important that authors explore all of the options that are available to them when it comes to getting their book published. They should be especially aware of the rejection that is predominant in traditional publishing so they don't allow it to affect their confidence.

When things don't go to plan, whether that be through rejection as an author from a publishing house or you're facing challenges along the way, self-confidence is the single most important factor you need to succeed as an author. Especially since good writing is not a quick and easy process. No matter what avenue you choose to publish with, it will still take time and energy.

I know from experience that writing requires a certain level of energy, discipline and optimism, even on the days where you make little to no progress. Our confidence can be tarnished when we feel blocked or burned out in our writing ability and it's important to be able to recognise this to regain control in these moments before our confidence is shattered. The problem is that when you're writing a book, the hard work that goes into it isn't instantly appreciated. In many ways the gratification from the writing is delayed. That in-between time can also shape our confidence, but it doesn't need to be this way.

Here are just a few ideas for you to ponder within those moments of losing your own self-confidence:

Stay Connected

Writing can be a very solitary task. Maintaining contact and accountability with other people is really important to avoid the feelings of loneliness and isolation that can come with the territory of being an author. A few positive words of wisdom from others can go a long way when it comes to maintaining your confidence.

Keep Going

Even if you are struggling with your writing, the most important thing you can do is to keep going. "If at first, you don't succeed, try and try again." What may feel like a massive writer's block (which I will talk about later in the book), may just be the need for you to take a break, give yourself a 'check up from the neck up' and get back to it. It's OK to delete work that you're not happy with. It's normal to write rubbish, especially in the first draft. If you are doing this, you are normal. It's part of the process. Again, it shouldn't be something that knocks your confidence.

Go back to your goals

If you feel like you are losing your 'mojo' and your confidence along the path of publishing, one of the greatest things you could do is revisit your passion for why you started in the first place. Remind yourself of your mission and know you have the power to make it happen.

Ask for help

Never suffer in silence! Ask for support from friends, professionals, and anyone you feel safe with. 'A problem shared is a problem solved' after all.

Be Patient

If you are still desperately waiting for your big break with a publishing house, then be patient. You know this takes time. At this stage, it's a good idea to look at every option available to you, especially if you are keen to get your book published into the world sharpish!

My final advice here is, never let the rejection of publishing houses prevent you from pursuing your dreams. There is so much opportunity to get your book out there so never lose your confidence in YOU.

If the core of who you are believes without a moment's hesitation that everyone has the right to be successful; that everyone has the right to share their story; and that a life spent seeking approval from others is a life spent without joy, then please, stop sitting on your dreams. Become the woman that aligns with the empowering quotes you share.

You do not need to wait any longer, lovely. Please write your book.

2

THE BLISS OF A "BUSINESS BOOK"

NOW IS YOUR TIME

*I*f you are writing a non-fiction book that isn't for business purposes, stay with me. I just need to speak directly to those wanting to grow their business off the back of a book for a moment.

The idea of writing your very own book can be a daunting thought process. I totally get it. The sad truth is that only 5% of business people actually become authors even with the same opportunity in front of them. It is these people who overnight become the influencers, change makers, and go-to experts, elevating themselves above their competitors, especially in the ever-growing online space. When you stand out above the noise in this way it plays a huge part in your future success.

So, this is really about asking yourself, are you happy to play small and miss out on one of the very best marketing tools you could create? Or are you ready to become part of the 5% who create change in the world? I know for me, it would always be the latter, but let's dive into this from a few more perspectives.

When you allow yourself to play small, what you are really projecting is that you don't take your business seriously. Whether you are working part time, full-time or in the nooks and crannies of the time you have available, it is still a real business. One that deserves to be spoken about and recognised with authority and confidence. It's not a 'hobby' on the side that you are sometimes passionate about. It's something you have crafted your skills to learn, invested your time and knowledge into creating and mastered the foundations to be someone of great value within your niche.

It doesn't end with you though. How you play and show up in your business will also influence your customers' experiences, and whether they are going to refer you to the next person... or not. The power of referrals shouldn't be taken for granted. Referrals have the potential to grow your business *exponentially*. The bottom line is, if you take your business seriously, if you show up and be bold, you and your business will be taken seriously too. Your book is just a stepping stone to this...

Let's talk about the fear associated with this, one I can completely appreciate.

I know that for many entrepreneurs, especially in the early stages of your business, stepping up and taking BOLD action like writing and publishing your very own book can be scary. The thought of attracting the next BIG client or life-changing opportunity can actually paralyse us from taking any action at all. Let's flip that for a moment. How would you feel if you never achieved that big goal, big vision, big client or big opportunity that you see for yourself and your family?

I don't believe you started a business to play small and float in shallow waters. You have a vision, a purpose, a passion, skills and a wealth of knowledge, expertise and experience that only you know how to share. In turn, this will bring you and your family the life you sought to achieve. The magic of writing and publishing your very own book is the stepping stone to show the world you are fully committed and ready to serve with mastery in your niche.

This brings me on nicely to my next perspective.... being the expert. When you have a problem that you are looking to resolve, do you look for the person who has many solutions to many problems, or do you look for the expert who solves your current problem with trusted results?

Unlike the expert, the amateur will try and bridge the gap between many problems with many solutions, limiting them on achieving any tangible and solid result. This can confuse not only the way you work but also your audience and followers who won't have a clue what it is you actually do. Remember, a confused mind never buys and trying to market with multiple dimensions won't warrant any tangible results. So be the expert. Offer a solid service that solves a specific problem to a specific group of people.

So, what is the best way to share this expert knowledge and services? … In a book, of course!

You will come to find that one of the most powerful advantages of writing and publishing your own book is the power and confidence that it brings to you on a personal level. Instead of masking behind the unwritten rules of social media and marketing, your book will allow you to be unapologetically you, speaking your voice, your language, with your values. With so much noise and expectation in the online space, would it not be liberating to have the opportunity to JUST.BE.YOU?

You: the one who speaks directly to your ideal client in a way that only you know how, attracting those you are meant to be working with. When people have a problem they are willing to pay to solve, and they find the expert who solves their problem in a way that they know, like and trust, then you have a scalable business.

My final note here ends with you and your confidence to charge your worth.

It's true, especially in the early days of business, that many of us struggle to say no, charging prices that devalue who we are and what we deliver. When we come from a place of wanting to 'help' and 'support' people, mixed with the fear of playing safe to avoid out-marketing ourselves, we do not charge our worth. I too have been guilty of this and it ends up feeling like we are working tirelessly but not getting paid our worth. They say entrepreneurs leave 40 hours per week jobs to work 80 hours a week to avoid having a boss. I know this is true for many, but I don't believe it should be their reality. The truth is, it doesn't matter how many years you have been in business or what size your business is, it comes down to quality in what you are offering. Your book is the key to giving you the confidence to charge your worth.

When you step up, put yourself out there and become an author, it will continue to serve you forevermore in business and in life. So, is the fear of writing and publishing your own book really worth sabotaging a lifetime of success?

THE BURNOUT EPIDEMIC

*T*he raw, unfiltered truth about the journey of an entrepreneur is one of both sunshine and storms and that's putting it lightly. When they say success is never a straight road, they really mean it. There will be many of you reading this who have experienced your very own trials and tribulations, lessons and blessings, successes and failures, all of which have cultivated the person and entrepreneur that you are today.

With the ever-growing developments in technology and competition, there is a real need to stay aware of the latest marketing and sales techniques in order to keep ahead of the game and above the noise. More and more people are becoming opportunist, taking advantage of the benefits associated in the entrepreneurial world, to create something for themselves. I am going to assume that's you too right now.

We all start with a vision, a purpose, and a passion. We take risks that most people wouldn't dare to, we push ourselves outside of our own boundaries, work long hours and continue to justify our crazy schedules in order to see our BIG vision come to fruition. At the same time, there is no doubt about it, being an entrepreneur creates freedom like nothing else can, with a lifestyle to match. It allows us to make our stamp on the world and pursue a fulfilling career where we can write our own pay cheque. Nothing beats having a vision, a passion, a purpose, and a desire to create something of your own to make the difference you are here to make. That's what makes you an entrepreneur. I know for me, I wouldn't be the woman I am today without my journey to success and for every part of that, I will be forever grateful.

To survive the journey, it's important for us to take responsibility and ownership for how we feel, work, respond and cope with the rollercoaster ride that it is. When we are feeling uninspired, unmotivated and frustrated in business, quite often we start feeling paralysed to take any kind of action, doubting our abilities to achieve, being incredibly hard on ourselves. Contrary to that, having the good days, the wins, feeling like you have made a difference, getting results and having a solid income can bring us back to a place of flow once again. However, it's not to say these wins haven't taken some blood, sweat, and tears to make happen – all of which physically, psychologically and emotionally impact us.

So let's face the problem head-on. The Burnout Epidemic.

You may not realise this but as you positively look for solutions when everyone else sees the problem, and you take advantage of opportunities which others see as obstacles, you are at a higher risk of burnout than any other group of people, and it's a growing epidemic.

Burnout can start by simply feeling like you have lost motivation, feeling exhausted, and anxious about your business, causing you to struggle to focus or sleep and finding it near impossible to make decisions. It's actually a form of depression, so it isn't something to be taken lightly.

Let's look at the realities of day to day life. No one tells you it's OK to have a break, so we don't, or if we do we feel guilty about it and never quite switch off. We have a responsibility to make everyday decisions, our income, our clients, our action.

Unless you are a master of setting your own boundaries and managing your time consistently around all of your commitments, you will be working at the risk of burnout as you struggle to find that work-life balance. It doesn't stop with how we show up behind closed doors either: we are continuously trying to keep up the facade of high energy, confidence, and success. This in itself can be draining at times, especially when we are craving some 'me' time. I would love to tell you that as your business and finances grow, the pressure stops. It does if you build it in a certain way, and that is certainly how I have built my many businesses for me, but for most, they continue to experience the heightened pressures of showing up, getting results, and achieving the next big goal.

Many people won't even realise they are experiencing burnout until it's too late. This certainly was the case for me when I realised my time was more precious than any kind of income. After having my little boy, Ted, I realised I had missed out on much of the early days of his life, and I made a commitment I would never do that again when Polly came along. My burnout (along with a whole heap of online bullying – but that's another story) led me to take a year out of business. The beautiful thing, though, was that I had created solid foundations which enabled me to take a year out, look after me, be with my family and still earn and scale my business in the background. This is what I wish for you too without you having to experience burnout in the process.

Wouldn't it be nice to have an automatic system working for you in the background that pays you while you sleep? The truth is, you can create something far bigger than you have imagined for yourself, without the need to work yourself into burnout, and instead allow the power of automation with your book to take over. A system that means you're earning an income, serving people, building a know, like and trust relationship with your ideal clients, and setting the foundations to set high-end sales all without the need for you to be present or consistently having to show up.

Your book becomes this key source of value and will continue to work for you in the background. This is what real freedom in the life of an entrepreneur is all about. It will help you get your message and service out there to a much wider targeted audience whilst bringing you a consistent income month in, month out.

So yes, it's time to step up to create that vision for yourself, but it doesn't mean burnout. It's about taking advantage of the technology available, cultivating your message in a book, and leveraging your time to grow and scale your business and income to its highest heights.

Your book will do the work for you.

YOU'RE LOSING INCOME

With any business venture, there will always be a certain element of investment. I know this can be daunting for many entrepreneurs, especially those in the early days of their business or those who have made investment decisions in the past that haven't paid off. You have probably heard the quote many times before that with a business it's important to "speculate to accumulate" and this can be part of any financial investment. My dad, however, puts it a little bit better. Allow me to share with you a conversation that took place a few years ago whilst chatting to my dad about "risk."

On showing my dad my business financials, I felt like I needed to 'come clean' about a £12,000 investment I had made in a mentor to support me with both my business and my very first book project. I used the words, "As you can see, I've taken a risk, but I know it will pay off." – He looked at me baffled.

"What risk?" he asked me.

"What risk? Did you miss the £12,000 gamble in those figures, Dad?"

"Abi, I repeat, what risk? You haven't gambled on a horse; you have backed yourself. The beauty of an investment in yourself is that you get decide whether you win or lose: you are the only horse in the race."

Those words changed my life. (Thanks, Pops!) I get to decide; I get to choose whether I make it work or allow it to fail; it's a choice, and I choose to win. You get to choose to win too.

However, all of that said, with a book we can be confident in the income opportunities that are there for the taking. I want to get super transparent with you so you can see how you too can use them to your business advantage.

There are various forms of income we can generate from a book, some of which include the royalties from book sales, continued purchases of your services, workshops, VIP days, retreats and speaking events just to name a few. I want to dive in deeper with these areas of income as well as some key elements for you to consider when deciding if you should invest in publishing your book.

My goal for you is to become published, positioned and really flipping powerful within your industry so let's first touch upon 'why publishing?'

Impact

The impact that you can have with a book is so vast compared to the impact you can have purely by focusing on social media type outlets. As business owners, we want to put our adverts and funnels out there for maximum impact. We want to get our message on social media because we think that's where people are hanging out 24/7, but that simply isn't true: only a tiny percentage of your audience will be seeing your offers and updates. Whilst many of the social media platforms are used, Amazon is actually the number one marketplace in the world. My question to you is this: why wouldn't you want to put a piece of yourself and your business on there so that people can find you, learn more about you and buy more of what you have to offer? Imagine creating something of value on the world's largest growing platform for people to access you directly. It's used globally so there really are no limits to how you can create impact with your work.

Industry Status

There is no doubt about it, when you write a book that focuses on your niche, your journey, showcasing your authentic voice, your credibility goes up almost instantly. Overnight you will position yourself as the expert and get so much recognition within your industry and this really is just the beginning. This new-found credibility opens up a whole new world of opportunities, the first one being to give yourself a long overdue pay rise! You are worth it, after all. You will become that 'go to' person in demand for speaking opportunities and guest expert slots before you know it.

Income

There are many avenues of specific income generated from your book and here I want to touch upon all of them. Personally, I have created so much success in the last six years because I have taken the opportunity of creating every income stream possible. Let's start with the obvious. One of the main methods of income is the royalties from the sales of your book, both kindle and print version. As we look at royalties in more detail later on, it is good to just be aware here that the percentage of royalties you earn does depend on the publishing route you decide to go down. With every avenue, however, there is always a royalty income for you.

If your book is created professionally for business (which I would highly recommend), you will also be able to lead people quite nicely into your programmes and your 1:1 offerings as a service based entrepreneur, and into your online courses and programmes. This is something I establish with my clients right before the book blueprint is even created so we have a very clear end goal and objective in mind for future sales. This allows your book to be utilised as the best business card that you will ever have. Make sure you establish this before putting pen to paper.

No matter what publishing route you decide to go down it will really serve you with your income goals. With your message getting in front of the right people there is so much opportunity for radio, TV, speaking events and opportunities on a global scale that before may not have been achievable. These opportunities can be the stepping stone to huge financial jumps within a business. I am proud to say that all our authors have made an impact in the media and on their income just like this.

I have previously touched upon taking advantage of automation within your business and this really can transform your income. Why not create a funnel for your book? We all know that creating a funnel on its own has the potential to take your business to six figures and beyond, so imagine how much more of an impact you would create with your book at the very front of that funnel. Being part of the 5% of the population who have a book as their front end offering and allowing your ideal clients to get to know, like and trust you before working with you, you are opening up an avenue for people to find you, work with you and to pay you for your services. This is not about the hustle anymore. This is about taking aligned action for results and publishing will help you do that.

The truth is, whether you choose to create a funnel or not, books don't need batteries – it's not going to run out. It is going to work for you forever and a day. That is powerful.

Before any of this takes place, many of our authors choose to organise a launch day, and why wouldn't you? It's an amazing opportunity to celebrate and showcase your phenomenal achievement, promote yourself online and get even more exposure in the media. Not only that but the sale of tickets can generate an income that pays for your initial investment in the first place!

I want to finish here, by focusing on how YOU have the potential to impact your income by writing and publishing your book. I truly feel that the personal experience and benefits achieved are just as important as anything else in the process. This is why…

Consider how you're going to feel when that book lands on your doorstep for the first time and you are holding it in your hands. Imagine knowing you are one of the five percent of people that actually publish. You will have so much confidence, self-worth and can be proud you are part of the elite. Your standards will automatically rise, and it will allow you to speak to people in a way that you haven't spoken before. You are going to feel confident in raising your prices and charging your worth. (Not that I believe any of us can put an actual price on that.)

So, as you can see, there really are endless opportunities

when it comes to generating an income with your book. I hope this has given you more confidence about making that initial investment to take yourself and your business to the next level.

3

THE MAGIC BEYOND THE STILL LIFE

STILL LIFE

 noun

The subject matter is inanimate and never moves, typically with a focus on household objects, flowers, or fruits.

— CONCEPT ART EMPIRE

The reason that we as humans are not invited to take part in a "Still Life" is because we aren't meant to be still. We should be living our lives moving and growing because that is how the magic happens.

Embarking upon the journey of authorship is one of both personal power and enormous self-doubt, but we cannot allow the little voices inside our heads to stop us from experiencing life's potential to its fullest.

The process of stepping up and allowing yourself to be seen in the way that your book will allow you to can be a be pretty terrifying thought… I know! This is especially true as we are all at different stages of our life and business. So, the question really is, when is the right time to be bold and publish your very own book? Is there even a perfect time? Do we need to wait until we have achieved that one big goal? How many years in business should you wait before you qualify to publish your own book? These misconceptions and excuses are why so many people never allow themselves to step up and make it happen. The truth is, none of this really matters. If you are brand new in business, even if you haven't even set up the foundations for your business, writing and publishing your book will support you at any stage.

We spend so much of our lives caught up in the 'thinking', that it's too easy to convince ourselves that now isn't the right time. I completely appreciate what it feels like to spend hours a day comparing yourself to others, especially in the online space. It's all too easy to see the success of others and feel inadequate.

Do you ever hear yourself thinking, "Perhaps for them but not for me... they have achieved more, done more, seen more..." and the list goes on? Perhaps you're waiting for that big goal to be achieved, or your income to be at a certain level? There is never a right time for anyone. The only difference from one person to the next is the decision they make to either hide in the shadows or to step out and be bold. There is this misconception that doing something 'great' has been reserved for a small percentage of people who go on to live their dreams while we become their cheerleaders. My plea for you to consider here is this: you only get in life what you tolerate, so stop putting yourself down while watching others shine. Step up and trust you can do this. You never know, your book may just be the beginning of an incredible journey.

People will ultimately believe in you when you believe in yourself. So be the leader, be the example, create the path for others to follow. After all, influence is energy and your book will allow your mission, your cause, your service, and your beliefs to move people on a whole new level. The most inspiring person is not the one who is naturally gifted and excels in all that they do. It's the person who is able to overcome the fear of doing something and do it to the best of their ability.

As a mum myself, there is something more important to me than anything else and something I feel is relevant when it comes to the topic of moving out of the shadows to shine your own light. This is about leaving a legacy.

> *"If you would not be forgotten as soon as you are dead, either write something worth reading or do something worth writing."*
>
> — BENJAMIN FRANKLIN.

I absolutely LIVE by this quote. There is something so powerful about leaving your name on a book. Why just be a name as part of a family tree, when you can put your thoughts, your wisdom, your knowledge, and that powerful core of who you are into a book that gets passed down the generations?

Your children, your grandchildren, your grandchildren's children will never wonder who you were, what you were about and what you stood for. Your book will be there right in front of them. Your book will be creating a legacy that will go on to pay you long beyond the time when you want to take a step away from your business, and that is pretty powerful in itself.

So, if not for you, do it for them. Stop allowing other people to step up and be seen whilst you hide in the shadows. Be proud of you, be excited to showcase you and see how everything changes for you.

I WILL NEVER BE GOOD ENOUGH SYNDROME

*B*efore diving deeper into the book process, I feel it's important to talk about the many fears that first-time writers can experience. It's important to understand what they are so that for one, you know what to expect; two, you know it's completely normal and shouldn't be a reason you prevent yourself from making your dream of becoming an author a reality; and three, so that you can manoeuvre through them like you would the red laser beams in a Mission Impossible film.

Before even putting pen to paper, one of the most prevalent fears that comes up for people is in their ability, or lack of, to write their book. The "I'll never be as good as..." syndrome is one that can paralyse people from even beginning the writing process. I want to touch upon this now to remove any barriers or apprehensions you may be feeling towards writing your very own manuscript.

As human beings, it's in our nature to be hard on ourselves. Comparing the writing of famous authors from around the world with where we are today can be paralysing. I really want to give you some perspective on this, because like anything, writing is a learning process: we don't just get great at it. Let's look at JK Rowling, for example. She is now a world-class author who has written multiple New York Times Bestsellers. But the raw truth is she didn't start there. Although now a global success story, she was once a struggling mother before deciding to birth the incredible Harry Potter books. You see, she didn't just get great at writing, she had to spend years crafting her skills, and mastering her creative abilities and this was a continuous process.

If you allow yourself to compare your writing skills with where some of these world-class authors are today, you are going to find yourself very frustrated, encapsulated with a lot of self-doubt and limiting beliefs. You will find fault in what you do, question your ability to articulate your message, and waste time fishing in someone else's pond when everything you need is already in your own. The reality is, we can only start right where we are now. You cannot fail before you begin so give yourself permission to learn and grow as a writer, make mistakes, and find what works for you. You have your own unique story with your own strengths and a journey for your readers to be inspired by. You can only inspire your readers from a place of integrity and authenticity when you write your way, from your truth, speaking your language.

I want to touch upon self-doubt in more detail because this really is the anchor that can stop people making any kind of progress towards beginning the writing process. When self-doubt creeps in (which it will!) the unfortunate truth for many is that their future book becomes a "someday" project. 'When I have more time, when I have more confidence, when I feel I can write more creatively...' and "someday" never comes. You don't need to be great to get started but you need to get started to be great. That really is my motto when it comes to people getting started on their manuscripts. Sometimes you have to build something bigger than your own self-doubt.

Of course, there will be times along the way when you struggle to get into flow and write even a few sentences, which will make you question your ability. So, self-doubt may well creep in throughout the process, but know this: it is completely normal. You do not need to allow your self-destructive brain to take over. Just be OK that sometimes you will feel like a rabbit running straight into headlights. It will be tempting to compare your writing ability with those who have had years ahead of you in crafting their skill, but you don't need to focus here. Focus on YOU, your readers and your message to the world. No one can BE.YOU.

Remember, your people aren't really worried about how creative your writing ability is. They are more interested in your experience, content and your ability to take them on a unique journey. This is what writing is all about, not to try and be the best writer there ever was, but through articulating your contribution to the world in your own authentic, unique way.

I want to end this section with a perspective to help you knock this fear on the head. Think about the person you were a few years ago, six months ago even, and hold that image of who you were, your struggles and what you did to overcome them. I am positive there will be elements in your life that have shaped you and you have grown in, become more confident with and mastered through some failure or lessons along the way. This is exactly how you need to treat your book when writing that manuscript... the way you articulate what it is you want to say will come. Not every day will feel in flow and there may be days when your mind goes completely blank and that's OK too. The bestselling authors of the world have these days too, this I promise you.

So never let fear hold you back. Your mission, your lessons, your value are too important, and the world deserves to read about them.

I NEVER FINISH ANYTHING

*W*e are our own worst enemy at times. We find faults in how we look, behave and think. We see ourselves differently from how the outside world sees us. The words we use and how we speak to ourselves can often be far away from how we would tolerate speaking to anyone else, and yet we fully accept the negative words and take them on board. How you talk to yourself is powerful: be careful. One of the major limiting beliefs and fears that comes up for writers, especially in the early days, is the worry of never finishing writing the book. For some, this actually stops them from ever getting started and their unique message continues to stay lost in the world. This is criminal.

If you approach life with the mindset of, "I never finish anything so why should writing a book be any different?" then you will continue to keep yourself playing small.

These cemented words will actually prevent you from taking any kind of action even though you have every capability. It's a crying shame, as voices get lost and never get heard.

We need to challenge this fear head on and actually appreciate why it might be that you never complete any tasks. There may be some underlying reasons preventing you from ever following through in the past. These can be little things, from lack of organisation, internal limiting beliefs or perhaps you are trying to be the 'Jack of all trades' and 'master of none' which leaves us feeling fragmented in our focus and where we need to be dedicating our time and energy. I know for me it's been my planning and ability to dedicate time to one thing at that moment. As busy entrepreneurs, it's all too easy to fall into the trap of going from one thing to the next. Living in this place eventually causes burnout and exhaustion emotionally, physically and psychologically.

At this point it's important for you to take the time to reflect on why you might have struggled to follow through in the past. It's no good going out into the garden and convincing yourself there are no weeds. You need to find the weeds, dig them up and get rid of them, and sometimes this takes some reflection and reality checks on where you are. I promise you, this exercise isn't just going to be invaluable for your book writing process, but equally for every aspect of your life in business. Awareness in itself is more powerful than anything else: becoming aware of what has potentially been stopping you will support you in flourishing to the next level, whatever that might be for you. It's time to change the story that you tell yourself. If you have never completed anything, start with something small and see it through until the end.

Let's direct this thought process towards our book. As busy entrepreneurs, it's all too easy to fall into the trap of going from one thing to the next. The truth is that writing takes focused time so being realistic with yourself is imperative.

Yes, I know. Starting a book is hard. Finishing it is even more difficult. But you will come to find that part of the book process requires something we call your 'Book Blueprint'. This is your plan broken down into manageable bite-size chunks. Writers who spend time preparing for what they are going to write have a much higher probability of finishing what they started. Part of this process is going to require you to take the time to create your blueprint which will form the foundations for you not only getting your book started but finishing it too. This is essentially a brain dump of all the ideas for your book that you can then put in an order. It will help you identify the chapters and sub-chapters and within each, all the points you wish to talk about.

I will come on to talk about your book blueprint in much more detail in future sections but from the 'getting it finished' perspective, be reassured that from this point onwards you will have a map of your book that's easy to follow and implement before even getting started. You will have planned ahead and brainstormed all of your ideas and have a clear outline to move forward with. So, if you fear not finishing your book, you really have nothing to fear at all. If you get the preparation part right, you will be set for publishing success.

Don't be daunted by the thought of writing a 40,000-50,000-word book. Instead, remember this is going to be a project broken down into very clear, manageable bitesize chunks. All it's going to take from you is a little bit of planning and creating a schedule that is going to work for you. Perhaps your schedule allows you to dedicate one day a week to your writing, or perhaps you prefer small bitesize daily chunks? This is really about finding what works for you, what gets you into the flow.

Remember that progress equals happiness. When you can make even the smallest of steps forward by drafting that first sub-chapter, or creating a schedule, this momentum will carry you through. It starts with a decision to go for it and commitment to preparation with the end in mind. Focus on one step at a time and be sure to recognise your achievements along the way, no matter how big or small.

I believe in you; I know you can finish. So, it's about time you believed in you too.

THIS TYPE OF BOOK HAS BEEN WRITTEN BEFORE

*a*nother very real fear for many potential authors is the knowledge that your book, in some shape or form, is already out there. That fear that it's already been written, it's already had its time to shine and there is no room for your book in the marketplace. This can then leave us comparing ourselves with those previous authors. This comparison serves no one.

Fearing that your book isn't original enough is just an alternative expression of fear that leaves us asking disempowering questions. "What if I have nothing new to offer?" "Will my book just be the same as everyone else's?" "Everyone already knows everything I have to say... right?"

All these disempowering questions will affect not only your ability to write but the vision you have for yourself and for your business. Think about it: are you the first person to coach, teach or train in your particular niche? Of course not, but that doesn't mean to say that you share the same wisdom or knowledge as everyone else who also specialises in your niche, does it? The truth is, while it's understandable to feel this fear, the good news is that you're not on your own. This is a common feeling among potential and new authors. They have this misconception that for a book to be valid, it needs to contain some new-found knowledge or insight that no one has ever considered before now.

This is quite possibly impossible! Very few, if any, books are profoundly original.

Let's look at an example here. If you write mostly nonfiction, to be more specific, self-help books, at the moment there are over 200,000 books in the self-help category. But what does this actually mean? It means that there is a good chance that the book you are writing has hundreds of similar themes and competing titles. BUT there is one big difference: they haven't been written by YOU!

YOU: being able to articulate your knowledge in your own way, making it accessible and usable to your readers. So, if you can create something that covers a certain topic with your own unique perspective and it allows your readers to gain new insights into the subject, then that is valuable. Your way of thinking, feeling, and speaking may be what they need to put the missing pieces of the puzzle together in their world. How you go about creating this can, of course, be inspired by previous authors, their knowledge, and their experiences, but the core of what you are sharing and how you share it is ultimately down to you. Your unique voice will enhance your readers' experience to help them identify new ways of thinking, feeling and seeing. Remember, people will read what they WANT and NEED in a way that resonates with them.

Of course, there are always going to be books that cover the same themes, places of pain, solutions, and niches but each and every one is completely unique. Your experiences to date, life circumstances, lessons, blessings, trials and tribulations have all been unique to you. How you have responded and chosen to overcome some of these very things has been unique to you. How you articulate your words, the language you speak, the people you are looking to inspire and support are all unique to you. How you intend to leave your footprint in this world is completely and uniquely you.

Besides, lots of competition can be a good thing. It is all confirmation to you that your topic, niche or area of interest is one that is popular and sought after, so instead of looking at this and fearing it, challenge yourself to step up and be better than what's already out there. If you scroll through Amazon, you can see thousands of titles in every kind of niche and category. Take a look at the books in your niche and ask yourself, "How can I do better? What are the gaps I could fill in?"

Remember that you are a unique individual. This means

your writing and voice are unique to you. Your book will enable you to discover your voice through writing and packaging your book with a killer cover, compelling book description, and a striking title. Of course, utilise whatever is already out there to inspire you, guide you and help you formulate the foundations for the message you want to bring to this world, but don't allow it to dominate. It's time for you to discover your own voice, one that will resonate with your readers in a way that only you know how. So, look at the gaps, see what is already out there: what else can you deliver that brings your book that unique selling point?

Perhaps you need to give yourself permission at this point to remember your journey and recognise how you have arrived at where you are today. It didn't just happen; there were steps that had to happen along the way. Perhaps this path is exactly what your reader needs to hear? Never be afraid to share a part of YOU in your teachings. That's why your book is and always will be unique.

I DON'T HAVE TIME TO WRITE

*L*et's keep this one short. We all live in a world that's becoming more demanding both online and in the offline space, and yet how we spend our time is ultimately a choice.

The truth is, we all have the same 24 hours in a day. The same 24 hours that Serena Williams used to train and win 23 Grand Slam titles. The same 24 hours that Vincent Van Gogh had to create his artistic masterpieces that would be forever remembered in history. The same 24 hours that any one of us can use to achieve any goal. None of us is able to make more time, but how you use your time is completely down to your own choices. If these people can achieve greatness in the same time that you have available, why can't you? These people recognised the value in every 24 hours and didn't waste time on the things that didn't really matter. They focused precisely on where they were going and the commitment it was going to take to get there. It was an unquestionable commitment because the outcome was, in their eyes, a done deal before coming to fruition.

I completely appreciate what it feels like to live in a busy world. Being a mum of two (with another on the way!), an animal owner, sister, daughter, granddaughter, wife, and entrepreneur, life can feel pressing at times... I know. But I always get done what I say I am going to get done. Why? Because I choose to. That really is all that time is about: a choice. Choosing to watch TV or spend an hour writing, choosing to browse on Facebook or focus that time into creating your next sub-chapter.... see where I am heading here?

Time is such an easy commodity to be used as an excuse when it comes to achieving anything. Sometimes there is much more behind this than meets the eye and perhaps you can relate to this. Have you ever said that you haven't got time for something, when the truth was you were just too paralysed with fear to do it? Writing a book is just the same, especially if you have never written before. The thought of sitting down to write is stressful. We are blinded from knowing if we are going to be able to articulate any words on paper or not. Using time as your cover-up excuse might make you feel better in the short run, but in the long run, it will never go on to serve you. So, my message here is if you have allowed time to be your excuse, what is the real reason you are keeping that excuse alive?

Quite often it can come down to an individual's perceived writing ability, or lack of, I should say. You need to remember that writing ability comes with practice and you'll never know how talented you are until you decide to try and write, and you will only get better by writing. As they say, sometimes you just need to eat that frog!

Another sad reality of time is that it's often about self-discipline. We are living in a world of constant distraction and with almost everyone moving into the online space, our world can very easily become filled with pressing emails and notifications. With little or no self-discipline, this can cause many entrepreneurs and professionals to waste hours a day surfing the net and achieving nothing. Sometimes we are not even aware of it. You make time for the things you choose to make time for. If you claim to not have enough time for something, it just means it's not that important to you right now. If this is you, perhaps you need to consider why writing a book is important to you in the first place.

Don't forget where your book has the potential to take you. Too often I see people giving up on their dreams because they would rather accept comfort in the short term and avoid pain, than experience short term pain for long term success. Nothing will change unless something changes. And I promise you this, when you make the first step and create that first bit of time to get started it's like ripping the plaster off. It's painless and will give you the momentum to keep going.

Fitting the writing of a 40,000-50,000 word book into your busy schedule seems really daunting. I want to make this simple for you and break it down to the reality of time.

- Your book will be broken down into, let's say, 10 chapters of 4000 words each.
- On average it's going to take you about ninety minutes to write 1000 words.
- In forty to fifty days, at 1000 words a day, you would have your first draft ready. In 60-75 hours of your life you can have your manuscript ready.
- Writing 1000 words a day is the equivalent of writing a blog post, that's all.

So now do you feel like you could plan a suitable writing schedule into your life? One that fits in the nooks and crannies of the spare time you have? Of course you can! I put it to you that this method has successfully created over 250 authors that I have personally supported since 2017.

Remember, you're not on your own. I will be the best accountability buddy you could ask for. Don't let time become an excuse, use it in the best way possible for you.

WHO WILL TAKE ME SERIOUSLY?

I used to think that in order to be taken seriously you had to have a PhD. Or be the CEO of a large company. But the fact is, most readers don't care about this. They don't want credentials. Rather, they need a story to be entertained by, or a book that improves their lifestyle. You make someone have a great day or give them the tools to forge a better life through the material in your book, and that is the only authority you need. You will have done your job as an author.

You really can make a difference wherever you are on your journey. You may not be famous or have a degree in writing, but you can sure as hell share your journey and what you have learned along the way to positively impact someone else's life. Your unique journey may actually serve someone more powerfully, because as human beings they will be able to relate to it as they are nearer to where you are as an author – this is powerful! When the reader can relate to you on such a level, they will become so much more inspired and feel so much more value from what has been written.

When writing, you continuously want to be reminding yourself that this book, although based on your experience and knowledge, is not about you, and much more about your readers. Ultimately, it's their lives that will be impacted, their businesses that will benefit, or their situations that will improve because of you.

When people find value in something that positively impacts their life, they may not necessarily remember who said it, but they will always remember how something made them feel. This has nothing to do with an author's credentials. It's about your ability to write something that means something to them, that emotionally engages them on a level that means they take the action to positively change something in their life.

Being you is more powerful than any credentials after your name. Your vulnerability, authenticity, and ability to emotionally touch people is what will create the most powerful read. The moment you feel you might possibly exposing too much of your heart and truth inside the cover of your book, is the moment you will be getting it right. In the end, it all comes down to your story. Emotion will always outperform any science, fact or credential. So, don't go into your book thinking people will only take you seriously with more of these things because it simply isn't true.

And let's think about this for a moment: who really is the expert anyway? How many credentials does it take to be considered an expert? How many years of experience in your niche does it take? See my point here? Your book will be the foundation that positions you as the expert like nothing else can.

So, all I can say here is move out of your own way! The expert positioning will come after you're published.

When using your book for this, you can write with authority and make an impact. It's OK to source facts from the net to back up what you're saying; you don't have to 'know it all' before starting. Your main objective when writing is to gain that trust and this comes from being honest and writing with integrity. Your readers are looking for information around the topics they are interested in, so give it to them. Write what you know: your knowledge, experience and unique insight from your expertise in your topic area.

So, think about what you can use here. Have you created a system at work to improve productivity? Do you love animals and can teach people how to expand the life of their pets?

There is an audience out there that wants the information,

experience, and guidance that you have and is willing to invest in your book.

Readers aren't interested in your credentials or awards. Give them something worth reading that will change their life. If you can do that, you become the authority in your field and people will pay for what they want.

I'M TERRIBLE AT SALES

*L*et's get right to the truth of this one. Yes, it's true that a writer is responsible for promoting their work to a specific audience. Regardless of whether you are a self-published author or under contract through a traditional publisher, promoting and marketing your work is part of the business. But you don't have to be a salesperson pushing a product you don't believe in.

Why are most people afraid of sales? Because they don't believe in or feel excited by what they are selling. Or maybe it's not "THEIR THING" they are selling but someone else's.

When it comes to marketing your own book, you will discover that selling it, although hard work, is fun. Why? Because it's yours. You believe in it. If you didn't, you wouldn't have written the book in the first place. There is no one else in the world that could be more passionate about your book than YOU. You know what it has taken to bring it to life, not just in the writing and publishing process, but having lived and breathed the very experiences you refer to in your book. There is no one in the world more convinced about the positive, life-changing impact you know your book has the potential to bring. So YES, you will find it easy to shout about.

And, if you have some extra cash to spend on a book promotion, then it's good to know that there are lots of services out there that will do the promoting for you. Phew! This is especially great for those who have limited time but are looking for a big number of sales.

The truth is you don't have to be a marketing guru to sell books. You just need a comprehensive marketing plan and to know where your audience hangs out. Growing any business teaches us these skills anyway and the key to over-coming the fear of selling is to get confident in your approach. Preparation is key and will go a long way when it comes to selling your book. It's like anything: fail to plan and you will plan to fail. So, think about your audience, think about where they hang out and create a strategy that you know is going to reach them and be consistent.

The secret to selling your book comes down to getting super clear on your ideal readers with a good under-standing of their wants and needs. Once you are clear on these, it will create the foundations for your marketing. Having awareness of your reader's pain points can help you articulate really powerful marketing strategies that enable the reader to A - see that you understand how they feel and B - have the answer they are looking for. There is never any need to convince. When someone has a problem and they are willing to pay to solve it, and you can show them you have the answer in a way that speaks to them, you have a sale.

Selling your book doesn't need to be an 'icky' process. There are so many methods of getting your message in front of your ideal readers to make a sale that it's just about selecting which approach feels more comfortable and is going to work for you. Not everyone is going to buy your book, so be OK with that. In many ways, as you start to sell, you will start to learn what strategies work and which ones don't. If you decide to go at this side of things on your own, just be willing to step outside of your comfort zone.

Later in this book I'm going to guide you through a full marketing plan, as well as doing a deep dive into your various marketing opportunities. So even if it feels a little overwhelming right now, trust that you will be guided every step of the way.

At the end of the day, everything we do in business eventually comes down to making a sale. It's part of living and breathing for most of us, especially as entrepreneurs. So don't over think it, stop being afraid of it and know there is an abundance of support out there to help you.

4

CHOOSE YOUR YELLOW BRICK ROAD

THE TRADITIONAL PUBLISHING ROUTE

*F*or the next few chapters, I am going to focus on the three types of publishing options and dispel some of the myths associated with each one. It's important to understand the pros and cons for each method so you can understand and appreciate fully which direction may be the best option for you.

All of this will support you in getting published, positioned and really powerful within yourself and your industry. So, our first stop… TRADITIONAL PUBLISHING. Let's look at some of the many advantages.

Prestige

There is absolutely no doubt that prestige comes with the territory of traditional publishing. For some of you, to be able to say out loud that you have been published with a publishing house may be your idea of success and publishing this way gives you that validation. When a publishing house chooses to publish your work, it shows that you are being recognised for the credible contribution you are seeking to make and for many that means more than any other part of the process.

No upfront financial cost

This really is where the term 'book deal' comes from. As my heading says, with a publishing house there are no upfront costs which eases any financial pressure in the publishing process.

Print distribution in book shops is easier

The publishing houses will normally have established long term relationships with many of the book shops and chains, meaning you already have your foot in the door to potentially get your book into shops with ease. Getting your book onto shelves will without a doubt support a high number of book sales too.

A professional team

The opportunity to work with a professional team who know exactly what they are doing at every part of the process can give you complete confidence and peace of mind that you will be putting out there a professional finished product. There is no risk of something amateur or 'shoddy' getting printed and this amplifies your confidence in the whole process.

So, as you can see, there are some real advantages of the publishing house option. However, it is important to be aware of the disadvantages of this approach too. So, let's take a little look...

It's an incredibly slow process

This is super important to understand and for you, as the writer, one of the first things to determine is how much time you have got before you want to be positioning yourself as the expert. Not only that, but how long have you got to create the impact you want to create, to earn the income you are looking to earn and to have the industry status that you deserve? When you are putting your manuscript out, or submissions out to publishing houses, the reality is it can be months and months, even years before you receive a yes. And it doesn't stop there. Once you then finally get that yes (if you ever get that yes), you are then looking at years before that book is available to buy. It could take anywhere between two to three years for a publishing house to put your manuscript into a book form that can be sold to others. It's a sad truth but one that needs to be understood.

Loss of creative control

What does this mean? Creative control is looking at how your book looks on the inside and the outside. When it comes to formatting and designing the cover, this, unfortunately, is out of your hands. So, when thinking about that cover you have had in your mind, the one you always envisioned for your book, you have no power as this is taken over by the publishing house. They will print what THEY are happy with so you need to be OK with not knowing how your book may look or feel and trusting the process and their creative control of it.

Low royalty rates

Previously we touched upon the income you will receive, which can vary depending on the route you choose to publish. Selecting the publishing house route, unfortunately, yields the lowest royalty rates for you. Traditionally with a publishing house, you would be looking to get anywhere between eight to ten percent which, if I am being completely transparent, doesn't equate to very much. You need to ask yourself if you are willing to allow that publishing house to take the majority of your royalties for each sale made.

A lack of significant marketing help

There is a real misconception that if you go with a publishing house all of a sudden your book is going to be heard and read by millions of people around the world whilst you are supported with a strategy for marketing. If only this was the case. Unfortunately, it's incredibly far from the truth.

A publishing house will absolutely expect you to take control of the marketing elements of getting your book out there. This is why lots of traditional publishing houses don't base their decision about whether they publish your book on the quality or content of your manuscript, but rather by looking at how many followers you have on your social media platforms. They are aware that they will not be spending a penny on your marketing and therefore need to be convinced you have a following to market to in order to make sales. Some of my own connections who have desired to go through the traditional publishing house route have had to build their social media followings to anywhere between thirty thousand and over one hundred thousand before even being considered.

Your book does not belong to you

This is an important note to be aware of. Once you sign a contract for your book, it essentially belongs to the publisher. All your knowledge, content, experiences, part of you and everything within that book will be signed over to the publisher. You need to decide, is this something you are prepared to do?

That encapsulates the many pros and cons with a traditional publishing house approach and I hope it has given you a clearer perspective of what you can expect. Let's move on and look at how self-publishing differs.

THE SELF-PUBLISHING ROUTE

*S*elf-publishing is a route opted for by many of those who want to keep control of the process. Just like the traditional approach, there are both advantages and disadvantages that I will uncover for you. First stop, the advantages.

Total creative control

Unlike traditional publishing, as a self-published author you retain the rights to keep complete creative control of both your content and book cover design. This is a real advantage for anyone who has a specific vision about how they want their book to look and feel. To be super clear, you get to decide the content – which doesn't have to be edited in any way – exactly what the formatting on the inside looks like, and your external book cover. It's all completely yours based on your decisions.

It's a faster time to market

With self-publishing, the whole process is much quicker because it is completely determined by you and the speed at which you wish to write. So, if you decide to start writing today, and you want to have your book ready in three, four or five months, then great! The control is completely with you so you can decide the time in which your book gets out to market.

Higher royalties

This is an important point to consider when it comes to the income generated from your book. If you are going to publish your book on a publishing platform like Amazon for example, the royalties will get split between you and Amazon. This normally equates to anything from forty to sixty percent of the royalties to you, which is considerably higher than going through a publishing house. So, if the income from the royalties is important to you, then self-publishing is a much better choice.

Access to the global market

Because you retain the rights to your book, you are not restricted who you can market it to in any way. This gives you the great advantage of reaching the global markets to scale your business to the other side of the world. This is a great advantage for anyone who is able to sell their products and services on a global scale.

Like any process, there are some disadvantages to self-publishing too, so let's take a closer look.

You need to find a suitable professional's help

With self-publishing, the responsibility of the whole process does come down to you. It is so important to find suitable professionals who can support you at various stages of the book process to ensure the finished product is professional. The idea of self-publishing a book is that you really don't want it to look like it's been self-published. Without involving professionals you run the risk of putting something out there that is going to look amateur. Some of the major areas of book development for which you should source professionals include editing, proofreading, formatting, a professional book cover and getting a professional launch system in place to take your book to market.

You will need a budget upfront if you want a professional result.

Because of the professionals required for various parts of the process, ultimately you will need a budget upfront to achieve professional results. Unfortunately, nothing comes for free, so this is something that needs to be considered before starting the book process.

It's difficult to get print distribution in bookstores.

When I say it's difficult to get print distribution into bookstores that doesn't mean to say that it is impossible. It is more challenging, however, because unlike traditional publishers you haven't built the relationship with them yet. With this, I want you to consider a couple of things. Firstly, what does that actually mean for you? If you think about it, when was the last time you thought you needed to go to the bookstore because you wanted to buy this book? I can't remember the last time that happened to me because Amazon delivers my books the very next day. I can be sitting in my pyjamas not needing to leave my house. This is the world we live in today. Amazon is the number one place in the world people go to purchase their books. So, I want you to consider, does it even matter if you can't get into the bookstore?

The second thing I want you to consider is this: if bookstores are majorly important to you, how prepared are you to build the relationship? Because that's all that publishing houses have done before now. You can go and do exactly the same thing, build the relationship and get your book in there. It's just that you need to start that process.

Again, I hope this has given you greater insight and understanding of what self-publishing can look like for you.

Next, what have I created with Authors & Co? Time to look at Partnership Publishing and what this means for you.

THE ALTERNATIVE - A PARTNERSHIP PUBLISHING ROUTE

*S*o, after understanding the advantages and disadvantages of both traditional publishing and self-publishing, I am so proud to talk you through an alternative and how Authors & Co have bridged the gap. Taking the advantages and benefits from both sides we have been able to create a platform that not only takes any hassle away from our authors but also enables them to achieve every benefit of the other publishing methods whilst avoiding some of the disadvantages.

So, what does this look like for the author?

An established and professional team to work with

Within our organisation we have the experts in every part of the book process from formatting and book cover creation to PR and media. We have you covered with experienced professionals who niche in these very specific areas and know how to generate the best results. From this, you can be absolutely confident in the knowledge that everything will look to the standard of a professional publishing house, if not better. You will also get access to me, and my years of experience in the entrepreneurial world. Together we cultivate your book blueprint and plan clear objectives each step of the way to ensure you achieve your desired outcomes and objectives. I come from a place of credibility when it comes to knowing how to get positioned and into the media. I am so proud to say that every author who has come through us has become a bestselling author and gained media opportunities. I have been regularly featured in the media including Forbes, The Huffington Post and Marie Claire. I will use my knowledge and background to ensure we achieve the best result for you.

Accountability

Accountability throughout the entirety of the writing process is such an important asset but one that can sometimes be overlooked. Why is this so important to your publishing success? You might have an idea, one that you are incredibly passionate about, and you can see the bigger picture of how you want to get this out there. But you may have NO idea how to formulate that into chapters, subchapters and a book that will deliver results. If you are writing a book for the first time, how you sell your services within that context may be a completely new concept. This is where I come in and help you formulate it step by step. Even with this plan, if someone isn't checking in with you regularly to see how you are getting on with the word count, the chances are you will fall into the same trap as ninety-five percent of authors who don't finish. We want to ensure that doesn't happen to you, like it hasn't happened to our previous authors.

Done for you service

As an author, in my opinion, the only things you should have to think about is writing the content that you want to put out there, knowing how you are going to market that content, and how this is going to create the impact and income that you are looking for. Everything else should be out of your hands. WE DO EVERYTHING. So as soon as you have finished writing your manuscript, we will check it, proofread it, offer amendments to it, and design your book cover with you so that you maintain creative control. We will do all the formatting inside the book to your specifications and ultimately help you launch the book through a bestseller campaign (all done for you!).

It doesn't stop there. In alignment with your book and objectives, we will support you in getting into the media and promote you in achieving the opportunities you are looking to create. This brings me on to one of our unique advantages.

Launch and marketing support

We don't just want to help you write a book; we want to support you in getting it out there to the masses. Because let's be honest, what is the point in writing if nobody knows that it's even out there?

Done for you PR

This encapsulates everything in terms of marketing and PR. Utilising your book, our partner company Chocolate PR, owned by Jo Swann, will seek to get you out into the media: radio, newspaper and TV. The opportunities are endless and can lead to much bigger and better things. We will support you in the media for a period of time even after your book has launched.

A service to suit your timeframe

I often have people come to me with ideas, asking what's possible when it comes to time? You want to launch in twelve weeks? Great. Six months? Yes. Equally you may have already written your book and you are looking for support in what to do in the next month. The beauty of how we operate is that we work by the speed of the writer and we have a team who work around you to make this possible.

So, as you can see, we have bridged the gap between what's missing from traditional publishing and self-publishing and made it into a package that allows our authors to be confident in the service, receiving a professional product and objectives achieved.

5

THE ESSENCE OF YOUR MASTERPIECE

STARTING YOUR BOOK BY STARTING TO WRITE

One of the biggest mistakes that first time authors make is starting their book by starting to write. As tempting as it is to open a new Word document and start your first chapter, maintaining a writing flow and articulating all your ideas onto paper will soon become incredibly difficult. If you think of a housing development, none of the physical building work takes place before a plan and structure is made, makes logical sense and meets all safety and legal requirements. This plan creates the foundations of the whole development, from heights, depths, materials, legal, and everything else that comes with the building work. This entire plan is created on paper first before any work even begins. If this didn't happen in the beginning, we wouldn't have safe structures for our houses. If you tried to build the four walls with no foundations or knowledge of how or where you were going, it would be a fallen house in no time. You need to think of your book in the very same way.

Although it might seem like a great head start to just get writing, I promise you, you will not end up with the book that represents your ability or that does justice to your topic of interest. Your book is there to teach a powerful lesson, tell a story, provide valuable insights and information that move people, impact people's lives, and make a difference. You want people to get from your book what is intended: all this needs to be part of the foundations and blueprint structure. If you just go ahead, start writing and hope for the best, you're actually more likely to cause damage to your branding and everything you represent, as people won't value your content like they should, and it may even leave your readers confused. Writing without structure makes it far easier to go off on a tangent, forget the point you were trying to make, and miss important details that would have been beneficial to the book. I urge you not to be the author who makes that mistake. You owe it to your book, your life's work and your investment in making it a reality.

Something else to remember here is knowing that your book will become part of you. It's a legacy that will remain for forever and a day so each part of the process needs to be respected and planning your book blueprint is one of the very first steps. It's what will create the foundation and brilliance for your book. The other great benefit of having a plan is knowing from the beginning what journey you are going to be taking your reader on. You can clearly see what lessons and blessings you will be referring to from your own life along the way, knowing how each chapter and sub-chapter will come together to formulate the overall footprint you wish to make in the world with your book.

You want to enjoy writing your book as much as you want people to enjoy reading it. By having a blueprint and a plan, not only will it help you write with more congruency, but it will help you write faster and with more ease. To write 40,000 plus words with absolutely no plan or breakdown is running the risk of becoming part of that percentage who never actually finish writing their book. Writer's block, a phenomenon that I am going to talk about later, is so common in the world of writing, and this is the number one cause for it! No plan, no clarity, no book. You want to remove the guesswork from all of the writing elements and take the time to create the plan that ultimately is going to bring you to your end goal and objective.

None of the authors who work with us will ever make this mistake as it's one of the very first parts of the process, but sadly I do see many authors writing without a plan and ultimately never producing the quality book they had hoped for.

When you invest in yourself to birth your book into the world, it deserves your time, energy and focus to get the foundations right from the start. Your book can only reach its full potential by doing so. So, treat the planning part as one of the most significant parts of your journey, formulating the foundations for everything that happens next.

TANGIBLE RESULTS

As magical as the process of writing your very own book can be, from a logical perspective there will be reasons that underpin your purpose for writing and it's really important to get clear on your objectives before you begin the writing process. Unless you know where you are going and what you want to achieve from the process, there is no way of directing your manuscript in the direction that creates tangible results. What I am going to take you through now are some real-life examples as to why some of the people we have worked with have chosen to go on and write their very own book.

Let's start with our business hat on. If you have a business, one of the main potential reasons for your book might be to generate leads into your business, allowing your income and business to scale. Your book is a fantastic way to generate traffic, whether that be to your website, blog, programmes, courses, workshops or even your live events. Your book can be written specifically in a way that talks about and references the places that they can go and find you. A great way to do this could be to guide them to your website, for example, and offer them a freebie there, or to direct them to your podcast and show them where to find it. The directions in which you can guide your readers really are endless and social media can be used greatly to your advantage here in terms of Facebook group communities. So, a lot of authors for business write books specifically so they can generate leads.

For others, it may be that you are looking to reach and inspire a much wider audience. Perhaps you have a message, teaching, training, and tons of valuable information that you are desperate to get out there on a much wider scale. Having a book on Amazon is THE BEST way you could do this. Remember, Amazon is the number one place people go and search for information in the form of a book, so it makes complete sense that if you have information that you want to get out there, you have a book on Amazon.

Taking our business hat off, it's important to recognise that this doesn't have to be just about business. This is applicable to all sorts of writing. Many of the authors that I have worked with have written for cathartic purposes. In these instances, they may have been through traumatic life events and experiences and they want to: firstly, take themselves on a journey of healing; and secondly, support other people who are going through the same adversity in similar situations, giving them light at the end of the tunnel. Writing from this perspective allows you to get yourself, your story and your valuable inspiration to a much wider audience.

Perhaps you are looking from a sales perspective, direct sales in particular. This entails sales of your book itself which will pay you automatically and also the sales that can be generated at the back of the book. This is something I have previously touched upon with the focus on leading people into products, programmes, and services that you offer. But let's not turn our nose up at the fact that you do get paid every time someone buys your book on Amazon: that is an incredibly powerful extra income stream that you can bring in to your household's family budget.

Let me give you an example. If your book was making a profit of £4 and you sold five books a day for a whole year, you would make an extra £7300 that year just for having a book on Amazon. Yes, we would need to look at the marketing of that; yes, we would need to give a lot of thought to how to get your book out there and not just be a best writer, but a best seller. But before we get to all of that we need to look at creating that bestseller formula to create that bestselling book.

You might be looking to raise your profile and gain more credibility in your chosen space, industry and niche. This is for someone who wants to be known and generate not just a raised profile but a more professional profile as well. Being able to say that you're an author or a bestselling author obviously helps you to achieve that tangible result. This is another big reason many of our authors go on to write their own book.

One of the final tangible results you can achieve by writing your own book is that you will establish yourself as an expert. If you are a coach, for example, and you are offering exactly the same service as another coach, somebody will be far more inclined to work with the coach who is a best-selling author than work with the coach who isn't. I am not saying that it's necessarily right, but I have seen this so much within the industry and it's just a fact that's true. The person with the bestselling book will be recognised as an expert because they were able to write about it. It makes sense.

So, as you can see, there are many ways that people are trying to get tangible outcomes from this. Whether that is in generating leads, reaching and inspiring a wider audience, making that direct sale, bringing that extra income stream in, or raising their profile and establishing themselves as an expert, these are the most common ways that I have seen.

An important point for you to consider if you are contemplating writing your book is to think about which reason would be your priority. Out of everything listed, which one jumped out at you? If you could get anything from this, what specifically would you want it to be? It would be highly beneficial to write this goal down and get really clear on it, because that's the end goal we would be focusing on.

Following this, you then want to consider what next four tangible results you would want to prioritise. You can then underpin the main result with the four elements underneath and from here have a super clear objective and goal for your book.

YOUR DREAM READER

*J*t's now that important time to think about target reader research. Don't worry, I know it sounds scary, but this process can actually be really simple and one that I want to talk you through step by step. Let's start with answering the obvious question: why is Target Market so important in creating the foundations for your book success? If you think about the purpose of having a best-selling book, it really is just that. It needs to sell well and sell a lot of copies. In order to get that status, we want to make sure that the content is something people are looking to buy before we spend our precious time and energy writing it. So before thinking about creating your book blueprint, or even considering putting pen to paper, it's important to start with reaching your marketplace to find out if it's something they want, need and would be willing to invest in.

So why does your world need your book? By your world, I mean the people in your immediate network or your extended network of people that you can tap into. Those that will potentially be your initial buyers. Why do they need your book? If you are trying to solve a problem, what is the problem that you are trying to solve? What is the information you are trying to get over? Is this information that they would really like or need to receive? This is why we suggest our writers really think about their target market.

Here is some simple advice to get you started. The first thing to do is put together a Google form. I love Google forms: they are so easy, self-explanatory and easy to use. They are also easy to brand so if you're sending it out as a company, you can put all of your branding, colours and logos in there. The point of sending out a Google form asking very specific questions is to make sure that you and your potential buyers are on the same page. You might have the best idea for a book in the world but if people don't want to buy it then it's not going to be a best seller.

If your book is for business purposes, it's important to consider whether this is something your customers actually want. If you have an existing group of customers or followers, you are at a great advantage because you can start with them. Simply asking them questions about the book you intend to write and whether they would find it beneficial enough to buy is a great place to start. I know this can seem a bit daunting because of the fear of them saying no, but trust me, it is far better to know this information from the get-go. Even if a small number of people say no, it doesn't necessarily mean it's a problem, it just might mean the concept needs tweaking and you have missed the mark slightly. If, however, you are getting some yes responses, the next question to ask is how urgently do they want it? Is this something they are looking for and need now, in the next few months or potentially the next few years? The answer to this will tell you if writing your book is something you should be getting on with imminently.

One of the things I encourage our authors to think about is sharing something unique. So many people take inspiration for writing a book by reading lots of different books, that they rarely come out with any original or innovative ideas. They're just regurgitating what's already out there. So, my question for you to consider is this: have you got something to share that hasn't been shared before? A knowledge bomb that hasn't been dropped? If you have, then that is such a unique selling point for you and all of this becomes the foundations for your book description, subtitle, and the marketing of your book. Think about what it is you're sharing, and how you can either make it unique in its content or the way it's being delivered. These little things all formulate the big things when it comes to your USPs so take the time to think about this.

This goes back to that ONE BIG PROMISE to your reader. You need to have articulated with precision what it is you want to do with them. If your reader is currently at A and your book is going to take them to B, what is that transition and journey that they are going to go on? And more importantly, is this transition or journey something they actually need or want to go on?

As you can see, there is quite a lot of work to do in terms of reaching your marketplace and giving some thought to those questions. I urge you to consider all the ways in which you can start reaching out to your target market and capturing this information. Like I said above, it could be sending out a form, or it could be arranging some small focus groups. It could be about having a few one on ones and micro meetings with people, just ten to fifteen minutes, or even just picking up the phone and asking them a few questions. It's not scary once you get started and I promise you that the information is going to be absolutely invaluable to your book.

BUILDING YOUR AUDIENCE WHILST
WRITING YOUR BOOK

*A*udience building as an author is a fundamental aspect to the success and longevity of not only your book, but also your future pursuits and services. I know for many authors, one of their biggest fears lies in the lack of audience to sell their book to and so in this next chapter I want to support you with a clear strategy that will go on to serve you in all that you do. Of course, like anything worth having it takes some effort, but I promise you will thank me for it.

This process starts even before any launch strategy begins and through doing so not only will you have an audience of buyers to support your launch, you will also have an audience of people promoting the socks out of it for you. This will support you in reaching new communities of people and potential raving fans that beforehand may not have come across you.

Not only that but having a loyal audience is something that can really support you with opening up new opportunities. As your audience gains valuable insights from you, they will naturally start promoting you as they see opportunities that align with your work. This means you don't have to be everywhere at once.

The key to all of this is the word 'loyal' because simply having an audience (any audience) won't be enough.

So how do you go about it? There are three key principles that you need to consider:

- Firstly, taking your audience on a journey.
- Secondly, creating content and aligning your messaging to speak to them directly.
- Thirdly, being consistent and showing up.

Take your audience on a journey

When you take an individual on a journey, you need to take them through every part of that journey with you. This includes the good, the bad and the ugly. Showing up every day with a 'perfectly created life' does not allow people to get to know the real you and therefore trust or believe in you. This part of the process does require you to become vulnerable, but I promise it will help your audience believe in you and what you do.

A good strategy for implementing this could be taking your audience 'behind the scenes' of your book writing/business: not just the surface stuff, but the real stuff so they can support you through challenging times and celebrate your wins with you.

Creating Content

Another consideration to think about is why people are on social media in the first place. Predominately, they want to be entertained, not listen to a forty-five minute training on a particular topic. So as well as being vulnerable, be fun and be social. Consider this when creating content.

One of the very best places you can grow an audience is through having your own Facebook group. Just like you keep things fun and interactive on your profile, create a fun, social environment in the group too – one that supports everyone getting to know each other. This is the secret to a successful community. This type of community will create a network of people ready to work with you, who want to read your book and are ready to write an amazing review for you.

In terms of content for your group, using a content planner is a great way to keep structured and to keep consistent. For example, you may want to run a themed day one day of the week, a live training another day, a story telling post another day, and perhaps lessons and inspirational posts on the other days. Once you have established what will work best for you, your audience and your niche, it's easy to plan months of content ahead of time and even schedule the themed posts to go out automatically. If you already have a blog, repurpose that content into different posts: for example, quotes, an interview, and emails to your list, inspirational posts etc. Don't make this any more complicated than it needs to be.

I encourage you to start thinking about what you care about, and what you know your audience will care about, whether it be business related or not. From here, you will engage your audience with both on and off topic related content. This is the goal because the moment people start to resonate with you, is the moment they become your super fans. Of course, your main focus needs to be on your book topic and how you specialise online, but having secondary topics will also show people who you are. At the end of the day, you are your brand; not your logo, YOU. So you need to be out there, you need to be visible and you need to be showing people that you care.

I have found that the most successful types of posts include story telling posts. These are the ones people generally never forget so bear this in mind when creating your posting schedule.

There are so many ways in which you can leverage the power of content online. You could give value in other groups, run Facebook ads, speak in other groups about your topic. Find the ways that work for you and do them every day.

Be ok with being 'marmite'. The truth is, sometimes people like a bit of controversy and whilst it's all too easy to get wrapped up in the need to please everyone, you never will and trying to is not worth the effort. Be OK that some of your content may repel people. For others it will resonate so much they will become your raving fans and that's who we want to attract. People who are just like you.

A final note on content creation is the importance of not training your audience to only like 'freebies'. Instead you want to be selling to them early (even if it is low ticket). If you get caught up with an audience who just expect free stuff from you all of the time, you will become stuck when you actually put out an offer or try and sell your book. Get your audience into good habits early on.

Consistency

The final element regarding building your loyal audience is the simple aspect of consistency. You need to approach this with the awareness that it may take you quite some time to build any kind of momentum. It may feel like you are talking to yourself for weeks, scrimping by with a few likes here and there. This is normal and you have to prepare yourself to keep going. It may take you three months, it may take you six months, or it may be quicker than that. However long it takes, it will only happen if you continue to show up.

Getting started is the hardest part. I will talk about it more in later chapters, for example the need for 'lead magnets' and an email list but for now it's about focusing on the basics.

When it comes to growing an audience, remember that the people you are connecting with and speaking to are real people with real problems. How you see them will have a huge impact on how they treat you so be loyal back and show them you care.

CREATING YOUR BOOK BLUEPRINT

I want you to take the time and space to give this section the dedication that it deserves because this is one of the most important sections of the entire process.

Your book blueprint is not only the skeleton of your book but a fabulous reminder of what meat you intend to put on the bones. It can be designed in such a way that every time you sit down to write, you know EXACTLY what you will be writing about with a word count guideline to keep you on track.

I am going to draw out a simple book blueprint that will make perfect sense to you and explain how you can use this when designing your very own. I feel the best way to show you is to give you a clear example of the book blueprint of one of our clients, whose book was written and published within six months and became an Amazon number one Bestseller.

CLIENT BLUEPRINT

Title – Cake Biz Success

Subtitle – How to start or grow a successful cake business

Purpose – To gain credibility as a cake business coach

Ideal Reader – Female; Professional woman with young children who is fed up and has found a love for decorating cakes; Age 32-42

Problems and Challenges – Lack of belief from partners and parents; Battling the nay-sayers who say it won't work as a proper business

I am going to – Remove barriers; Any woman can be successful! I will give her confidence and understanding of how to rise to the top

What is she searching for? She wants success and to know that it is possible for her

What is my ONE BIG PROMISE to her? She will have the knowledge to start or grow a successful cake business.

What are the questions she (and others like her) are already asking me? Pricing; contracts; marketing; business advice; how to make a full-time income

Chapter 1 - Empowering the woman to know she can do it with my help.

- Talk directly to her.
- Talk about my own credibility.
- Reality of the marketplace.
- Other barriers.

Chapter 2 - Mindset and Confidence.

- Why is mindset so important?
- Dealing with nay-sayers and mood hoovers.
- Starting to think like a businesswoman.
- Knowledge will give you confidence.

Chapter 3 - Ideal Customer.

- Why you need to identify your ideal customer.
- How to create your avatar.
- Where to find your ideal customer.
- How to speak their language.

Chapter 4 - Branding.

- Why is branding important?
- Finding your colour and season.
- Finding your style.
- Creating your collection.

Chapter 5 - Pricing and Consultations.

- Why is having a pricing structure important?
- Competitor analysis.
- Confidence in holding pricing conversations.
- Cake Consultations.

Chapter 6 - Launch and Marketing

- Why is marketing important?
- Online Marketing.
- Offline Marketing.
- Ideas for a launch plan.

Chapter 7 - Legalities and Formalities.

- Registering.
- Insurances.
- Contracts.
- Process Mapping.

Chapter 8 - Run this like a business.

- Why people fail in the industry.
- Hobby baker to a businesswoman (tax etc.)
- Bank Account.
- Accounts.

Chapter 9 - Challenges.

- We know that it's not always plain sailing.
- Difficult clients.
- Not enough clients.
- Customer expectations.

Chapter 10 - Ongoing Guidance and Support.

- The journey doesn't have to be a lonely one.
- Having a business mentor.
- Four powerful testimonials from women I work with.
- Why and how to continue with my support.

Right there is an example of a book blueprint, broken down into ten chapters and 40 sub-sections. This made it really easy for our author to portray exactly the message she wanted with her book, broken down into bite size chunks so that every time she sat down to write she wasn't wondering where she was going next. Every single sub-section became almost like a large blog post to her that she could write in a 90 minute sitting and would eventually form part of her overall book.

In this next section I want to help you formulate your very own book blueprint. You can do this when you consider these questions and points in relation to your very own book idea.

What is the purpose for you in writing your book? Is it for visibility, credibility, to gain more clients? Is it to create an extra income? What is the purpose that you are writing your book for? Remember: you want to focus on the main purpose, underpinned by four other purposes.

Describe your ideal reader. Who are they? Who do you want to attract? Who are you wanting to work with? Who do you want to sit down and read your book?

What problems and challenges are they facing? Your book needs to solve them. You need to be able to talk them through their challenges to help them with whatever they are facing right now: so what are they?

What is the book going to do for them? What are they searching for and are you going to be delivering it? What is your ONE BIG PROMISE to them? When you look back at the blue-print example I described above, and look at the one big promise, you will notice that that is the subtitle of that lady's book. The one big promise can be turned into the subtitle of the book so that reader knows exactly what you are going to deliver on.

List as many questions that you can think of that your ideal reader is asking right now. Give them the answers to these questions in your book.

Once this process is completed you can then really start to think about how the book is going to come together. Your book can be broken down into ten chapters, containing four sub-chapters in each. A word count to aim for could be 40,000 words for example, so let's break it down. With

40,000 words, and ten chapters we already know that each chapter is going to be roughly around 4000 words. When we break this down further into four sub-chapters we are now looking at 1000 words per section, the equivalent of forty large blog posts.

On average a sub-chapter of this length is likely to take you around 90 minutes, meaning that in just 60 hours you could have your manuscript complete. How manageable does that sound?

Here are some of my final thoughts. You need to remember that this is not definitive but is more of a guide. If one of your sections is fifteen hundred words and another just one thousand, that is OK. It really is just your guide to getting as close as you can to a forty-thousand-word manuscript, as we know this size is perfect for you and your audience. Ask yourself these questions: where am I taking the reader next? Do my chapters and sub-chapters make sense for the reader? Have I been precise enough with my writing or have I waffled for the sake of hitting a word count?

So, when you have planned this out by answering all those questions, I would suggest you pass this to your ideal reader. Ask them if the book makes sense from their perspective. They will be the best person to tell you whether your book blueprint is actually what you should be writing.

WRITING HABITS

*W*riters are infamous procrastinators. But you don't have to be. The secret is in creating a solid writing habit. Good habits will shape how your book progresses step by step and will also support you in enjoying the journey, as you will be consistently making great progress. What I am going to share with you now are some of the very steps that have worked for our own authors when it comes to writing and creating supportive habits.

Set your habit in writing

If you want to form the habit, you have to be fully committed. Not on the edge, not "I'm going to try," but "I'm really going to do this." If I asked you to put your hand on your shoulder for a moment. Now "try" and take it off. You either "do" or you "don't do". This is something you need to remember when you start procrastinating. There is no "try".

It is also important to write it down and post it somewhere you'll see it. What is your habit going to be, specifically? When and where and for how long and what will you do? Write it down, get really clear and remember you "do" or "do not".

Do it at the same time daily

It's best if you have a certain time of the day to start writing. I prefer early mornings, but you might like lunchtime, or right before bed. Just be sure it's a time when you won't be tempted by other activities. Think about the time of day where you are most productive and creative and block time out to focus on the task at hand and NOTHING ELSE. If it means getting up an hour earlier to clean the house in order to start writing at a particular time, then go for it. This might require a little self-discipline but once you are in a consistent routine your writing and progress will flow.

Commit yourself to others

It's crucial to be fully committed to forming this habit. To do that, it's best to not make it a private thing but to commit yourself publicly. Tell your family and friends, your colleagues, put it up on your blog, post to an online forum. Tell them exactly what you're going to do and promise to report to them on a regular basis. Accountability is a great form of motivation when it comes to writing so make this a priority.

Put complete focus on it for one month.

One of the keys to forming a new habit is focus. If you place your full focus on forming that habit, you're likely to succeed (especially combined with the other tools on this list). If you are trying to create a bunch of new habits at once, your focus will be diluted. Don't fall into this common but tempting trap. Really give all your focus and energy to forming this new writing habit. Remember, this is not forever: this is temporary to make your dream of becoming a published author a reality.

Find your motivations

What are your reasons for doing this? What motivates you to sit down and write? What will keep you motivated when you don't feel like writing? Knowing your motivations is important — and it's best to write them down. Go back to your objectives for your book, what outcomes you wish to achieve and then relate them to the emotional reasons you are doing this. How will you feel? How will it impact your finances, family, confidence, self-worth? Anything that means something to you, keep that close to your mind and visualise all those things on a daily basis. Trust me, this process is really powerful.

Set rewards

Rewards are great motivators. Do them more often in the beginning: give yourself a small reward after the first day, and the second, and the third, then after one week, then two weeks, then three, and finally after one month. Make a list of these rewards before you start, so you can look forward to getting them.

Look after you

This may sound a bit wishy-washy, but think about it: when you are eating good quality, nutritious foods, having plenty of sleep, taking time to de-stress and exercising regularly, you are able to focus more, have greater energy, and be more creative. Coming from a place of exhaustion and running off sugary, unhealthy foods can significantly affect how you feel, your level of motivation and your inspiration. When we feel good and are confident in our own skin, we action things from a different perspective. I'm not saying do anything radical here but just make better decisions and allow yourself the time to look after you, because you are the biggest asset to your book.

As much as I would love to say, do all these things and you won't get stuck, I wouldn't be being totally honest. Writer's block can still creep in and get to you, but luckily for you I am going to give you some of the best hacks out there to keep you on track in the next chapter. Together with these writing habits, you are setting yourself up for real success and an enjoyable writing journey.

WRITER'S BLOCK

*O*ne of the paralysing aspects of writing your own book comes down to the actual manuscript itself, especially if we have never done anything like this before. Focused writing does take a particular level of discipline and, of course, needs to be scheduled, but even with everything in place we can still find ourselves stuck.

Before you embark on your very own journey of becoming an author, I want to uncover some of the most powerful hacks to beat writer's block forever, giving you space and confidence to overcome any writing blocks you may encounter along the way. Some of these hacks are preventative strategies so I urge you to implement them even before putting pen to paper.

Let's take a look at these, one by one:

Change the time you write

I massively encourage routine and a set writing schedule at the same time daily – but if nothing changes – nothing changes! Sometimes a switch up in your routine and a shock to your system can support you to creatively put words onto paper. You may even find that there are certain times in the day where you are more creative. Work with a schedule that enables you to perform to your very best, and if it's not working, change it up.

Change the location you write in

For the same reasons as above, a change in scenery has the potential to spark those creative juices much more effectively. Think about taking yourself into areas where you feel relaxed, undisturbed and safe. I often find removing myself from environments that have the potential to distract me helps. At home, for example, we are surrounded with the pressing demands of housework, ironing, animals, kids and everything else that can take our focus away. Because we are daunted by writing in the first place, we can find reasons to prioritise those pressing jobs first. If this is you, my advice is to go somewhere quiet like your local library, somewhere where you have no choice but to focus on the task in hand. You will find that you achieve so much more from a solid two hours focused work in the library than eight hours of interrupted work at home. It might take a bit of planning but it's worth it.

Stop worrying about grammar and being a perfectionist

Right brain vs left brain! The first draft is about letting the manuscript unfold and take shape. Revisions and further drafts are for cleaning everything up. Don't stop your flow over spelling errors and trying to find the perfect word in your thesaurus. It's not the time! All this is going to do is make you feel like you are making little to no progress so don't worry about the details. There will be plenty of time down the line to get those sorted.

When in doubt – dance!

No, I'm not crazy, I'm all about raising your vibrations to attract what you desire like a magnet. When you feel like you are struggling, it can often cause us to spiral into paralysis. Looking for words and inspiration? GET UP AND MOVE. Hit play on a song that gets your body moving, your heart smiling and your feet dancing. Five minutes is enough to move you from blocked to bouncing. It's amazing what a flush of endorphins can do in your brain. Change your physiology, change your focus, change your flow! Magic, right?

Back to your blueprint

Before even starting your first draft, you should have created your detailed blueprint – follow it! It doesn't have to be written in order. Write the subchapter that you feel most inspired to write. You can blend it in later. Every time you complete another milestone in your sub-chapters it brings about more motivation and inspiration to push forwards. So, start where it feels easier and move on to the more challenging chapters as you go.

Turn off the digital distractions

Get that phone on aeroplane mode and close every tab on your laptop. One notification is enough to take you completely out of your creative flow. This is an important preventative method and one of the most important ones to implement.

Use the 'Pomodoro' Technique

Google it. Set timers & go, go, go: there's nothing like the pressure of a countdown to make you spew out sentences! This also prevents you from getting distracted during your writing time, because a deadline keeps you focused until the end. This also allows you to plan your breaks. Work a solid 20, 30, 60 minutes even, and then have some time out, which brings me quite nicely onto my next hack.

Get some fresh air

I appreciate writing can make you a hermit, living in a dressing gown, not showering for days – but that is just gross and not good for you or your creative sparkle. Get showered and get out for a walk to clear your head. Give yourself space to listen to nature, breathe in the fresh air, get the sun on your face and be grateful for where you are. This is also perfect to do to with a nice cuppa during your writing breaks.

Read something that inspires you

Take a break to read something written by an author you

love. Immerse yourself in their flow until you feel your own returning. This can often spark inspiration and ideas for your own writing. I don't mean you should spend hours and hours reading books and making little progress, but again, this could be how you treat yourself on your writing breaks.

Meditate

We hear about the benefits of meditating in most areas of business and life, if not all, and it's true. Allow yourself some calm focus – anything from sixty seconds to ten minutes will change your game. You will 100% be more productive when you are coming from a calm, relaxed mind, and a bit of self-care and love needs to be a priority.

So, there you have it: some of the best kept secrets to overcoming writer's block. Simple, I know, but please don't underestimate the power of each and every one. You will find that some support you more powerfully than others and that's OK too. Find what works for you and do everything in your power to give yourself the best chance of writing success. You do not have to be a victim of writer's block.

CREATING YOUR FIRST DRAFT

A major cause of writer's block is trying to make everything perfect in the first draft. You are not 'superhuman' and spending hours on your first draft trying to get each section perfect is just going to slow you down. This is where you sit down, you're trying to write, but you're also trying to edit at the same time. Sounds exhausting, doesn't it? This relates to what I call the creative brain versus the editing brain.

What does this even mean? Your creative brain is your right side of the brain's activities. This is the magical place where you get all your great ideas, normally inspirational subconscious ideas that pop into your head as you're going about your day. Sometimes these ideas can feel like they are jumping out of nowhere and can take us in lots of new directions.

On the contrary to this, the left side of your brain is the

more analytical side and this is what we use for editing. It's the side of the brain that kind of picks apart your words and tries to make them better. You will absolutely, 100% kill your productivity if you're trying to do both at the same time. Imagine trying to be creative while you are editing. It just doesn't work that way.

When it comes to your first draft, you only want to be accessing the creative brain. This is why I highly emphasise the importance of doing the first draft. With the first draft, you're just going to write down whatever pops into your head. You take your book blueprint and just try to flesh it out with a series of sentences or paragraphs.

You're not looking for grammar or spelling or formatting mistakes. Even if you're stuck on a certain point, it's okay to skip ahead and just get through this first draft. You just want to get the words onto paper.

You're not worried about it reading well, or if it resonates with an audience, because you're basically doing what Stephen King calls writing with the door closed. You're writing this book for yourself. No one else is going to see it so it's okay to really mess up and not have it read perfectly because you will trust in the process that it will get fixed before getting to the point of the final manuscript.

The second brain, the editing brain, is what you use when you start to work on the second and third drafts, and you really want to trust in the process here. You know that you got the words on paper in the first draft, and what you do in the second and third draft is clean it up and make sure that the ideas are flowing. Really, the whole point of your first draft is to just get it out, because this is a great cure to writer's block.

Why not try setting a deadline by which you have to finish your first draft? Or, if you find that lengthy deadlines don't provide enough motivation, try reaching a daily or weekly word count (e.g. thirty minutes a day or five hours a week). Don't forget to reward yourself for a job well done when you reach each milestone.

Here are our top tips to get you started.

Go to the loo before you begin

Sorry if this sounds too silly, but when nature calls it's no less distracting than when your mother calls; and unlike with your mum, you can't ignore the call or say, "I'll get back to you later, sorry." The secret of a first draft writing is focus and flow, so not even your own body should be allowed to interrupt.

Put your phone into aeroplane mode and unplug the internet

For some of you, this is surely the most impractical and annoying advice ever. What if something important happens and you're not reachable to respond? Just remember that the whole point is to be working FAST – so all we're talking about here is 20-30 minutes of unplugged quietness. Can you not unplug for just twenty minutes? I think you can. Challenge yourself to get used to that. It really makes a huge difference in your ability to focus.

Use simple words

Forget your fancy vocabulary. Later you can furnish language, searching for just the right words for the particular undertone you wish to convey. For the first draft, just use plain language.

Write in a series of short bursts

If you're anything like me, a countdown clock starting with as little as twenty minutes will get you going like a demon. So, set an alarm on your smartphone, and start typing! You will be amazed how far you can get with a twenty to thirty minute countdown. Try it!

By actioning all the above tips, you will build the momentum you need to get your book well on its way to completion. Remember, we want to allow our creative brain to work its magic here: nothing too serious, just relaxed writing. On completing your first draft, you are going to feel really accomplished, giving you the motivation to build upon the foundations and create something you are really proud of.

BETA READERS

*T*o put it simply, a beta reader is someone who evaluates a manuscript. It's an especially valuable step if you are planning to self-publish but can also help you in the quest to get an agent or publisher if you are planning on taking the traditional route with your book.

Why do we need beta readers? The fact is, we spend so much of our time on our own manuscripts that we can't see them objectively – no matter how diligently we self-edit. These can be some of the outcomes (there are plenty more):

*We create an expectation early in the book but forget to deliver on it.

*We describe events in a way that is clear to us but not clear to a reader who can't see the pictures we have in our heads.

*We leave out vital steps in our explanation and don't realise it, because we know what we mean.

*The characters in our books (whether fictional, or real as in a memoir or non-fiction anecdote) may not be convincing, because we know them so well that we don't realise we haven't developed them thoroughly within our manuscript.

A beta reader will read your manuscript on their own, and develop a personal response to it, uninfluenced by the opinion of others. The thing I love about this is that reading is normally a solitary pursuit, and books 'happen' in the mind of the reader. So, it's an authentic way to experience your book.

The best beta readers will give you a written report of their responses (which could be several pages long), and they often also make notes in the text to show their reaction to specific sections of the book.

Ideally, you should get at least two or three beta readers, so you can then weigh up their reactions carefully. The responses will possibly be very different. Don't be alarmed by that!

Don't imagine for a moment that getting support from a beta reader is an admission that you don't know what you're doing as a writer. Quite the opposite. It's the professional way to go.

Of course, you can opt for a professional beta reader, but if you are on a tight budget, you can also ask friends, colleagues and family to help you out by giving them a brief like this on what you would like them to do.

Be grateful

Your beta readers are doing you a huge favour by critiquing your manuscript. It's a commitment of their time, energy and talent. It might take them anything up to twenty hours to do the work (depending on the length of the book and how much of the report they're giving). That's a VERY big favour being squeezed into a person's busy life.

Be helpful

These are some of the ways you can make it as easy as possible for them to do the job for you:

A) Provide it in the format that's easiest for them to read. Ask them how they'd rather read it. Do they prefer a Word doc, or a Kindle or epub file? Give them what they want, within your budget and abilities, of course.

It's not hard to convert your manuscript to an eBook. It doesn't have to be beautiful, as it's not the for-sale version.

B) Allow them plenty of time if you possibly can. I aim for two weeks with my beta readers, although sometimes there are deadlines that compress the schedule. Negotiate with your readers on the time frames they can work with. Remember it could be as much as twenty hours' work. Allow for them to fit that in around life.

C) Give them a manuscript that is as "clean" as possible. It might be in an early draft, but still, re-read it yourself and give it an edit, fix the outrageous typos, etc. Make it as

127

pleasant to read as possible. An advantage of this is that you'll get feedback on more important things than typos.

Be sensitive

We are usually so paranoid about sending our manuscripts that we forget one important point: most beta readers are nervous too.

Critiquing someone else's manuscript, even if a person has done it a hundred times before, can be nerve-wracking. That's amplified for a first timer.

As writers, we're often so busy thinking, "What if they think my manuscript is terrible?" that we don't notice the beta reader is thinking, "What if I hurt their feelings and they lose confidence in their book? What if they think my comments are stupid? What if I'm not a very good beta reader?"

Look for ways to brief them that make it clear their opinion is valuable because it will be different from everyone else's, and therefore it is unique. Let them know you will be getting multiple viewpoints and combining them all – that helps take the pressure off.

Set the tone

The best way to minimize the risk of getting either cruelty or fluff is to set the tone yourself in your briefing.

You could try saying something like: "Please be honest about anything in the manuscript that isn't working for you, and please be as detailed as you can. I'd rather hear it from you now than from 27 one-star reviews on Amazon later. But if you notice strengths of the manuscript, please also let me know what those are and why you think they are currently working, so that I can be sure to retain and develop them in the next draft."

So, there you have it, the way to use a beta reader in the process of your book.

6

PUBLISHING PERFECTION

THE QUALITY OF YOUR WORK

*W*hen thinking about the quality of your work, the last thing you want to be putting out there is anything that speaks amateur or rushed. Whilst the context of your manuscript is important, the quality of how it is written simply can't be compromised. This is the case for any stake including time, money or deadlines and includes the spelling, punctuation, grammar, spacing, paragraphs, typeface and the story itself. We are only human, and even though you may have read your manuscript one hundred times over, there may still be mistakes. The brutal truth is, if you have issues or errors with any of these elements, your readers will spot them immediately, and it will shatter your credibility as a writer. The whole purpose of getting your book out there in the first place is to position yourself above your competitors, so failing to provide quality is damaging.

With a properly planned schedule ahead of writing and a solid commitment to when you write, running out of time should be a very avoidable issue. Life can get busy so if you do get behind on your schedule, it's about recognising this early on and ensuring you take the required action to get back ahead of yourself moving forward. If you are having to write under pressure, not only will the quality of your work be compromised but so will your ability to be creative.

If financially you are out of budget, a great way of ensuring complete quality in your work is to enlist some help from your family members and friends. Asking them to read through with a fresh pair of eyes and actively asking them to detect mistakes is perfect. They will absolutely be able to detect errors that you haven't seen yet. Make sure you let them know why you are enlisting their help and the importance of checking for the small things so they do not rush through the process. Remember the small things will impact the big things.

If you would prefer to seek the support of professionals with this, even if you need to save for a few weeks, or months even, that's OK too and will be worth the investment and time. More than anything it will give you complete confidence that your work is up to its highest standard and there is no risk of anything compromising that. Personally, I would always choose to seek a professional and invest in getting the job done properly over saving money.

How I think about it is this… Imagine picking your book up and being aware that on several pages there are spelling mistakes or big gaps between the paragraphs that should never have been there… it would feel disheartening, right? After all your hard work and the time you have invested in creating something that will be your legacy, to find it has errors… You would always find yourself worrying if your readers can see these mistakes, and you'll be waiting for someone to comment.

It isn't worth compromising the quality. When you go to publish your book with the absolute confidence that you have done everything in your power to produce a professional manuscript that will positively influence its readers, you will be thanking yourself for not cutting any corners.

There are plenty of professionals out there who can help you (including Team Authors & Co!) but if you're going at this independently make sure you do your due diligence in researching who has experience with your type of book and that they too have the credentials to do your book justice.

EDITING & REVISIONS

*L*et it breathe.

The editing and revisions process means we are nearly there! Phew!

As we come into the final aspects of the book process, making time for these processes is vital. So, I want to now talk you through the simplest way to look at the editing and revisions process. I know it's a tedious task, but one of the most important nonetheless. So, let's rip the plaster off and jump straight in.

Like any author, your emotional attachment to your writing is strongest while you are working on it, so a short absence will allow you to reflect on the work with new, less sensitive eyes. The first thing I would encourage you to do is print out the pages, settle into your favourite reading chair, and write notes in the margins as you read through your work. Mark things that work, things that don't, and any additional ideas; if so inspired, free-write on the back of the final page and begin expanding ideas on the spot. Use colours, highlighters, and anything else that will to support you in making clear notes to refer back to.

Do not be discouraged if your first draft isn't up to the quality of your vision. That's what revisions are for so just embrace the fact that you are going to need to make some changes.

At this point, it's important to elicit a new perspective as you read through. You can use the insights and answers to some of these key questions listed below in helping you to create your revisions moving forward.

These include:

- What's your point?
- How would you summarise the storyline or argument of this piece?
- Have you cited your sources? Are your sources credible?
- Would additional sources strengthen your evidence?
- Who is the intended reader?
- Is the voice appropriate for the material? Does the voice remain consistent throughout?
- Are your ideas cohesively presented and

structured? Are there sections? How do they frame the piece?

- Do the ideas in each paragraph and sentence flow together?
- Is there resolution?

The answers to these questions will be a great starting point for making some positive and considerable changes to your manuscript. Of course, your opinion alone isn't enough, so the next fundamental part of the process is to seek feedback on the above. These could be fellow writers, editors, colleagues or even friends. Their perspective and feedback will help you get even clearer on the editing and revisions to be made. Ask them what is working, what isn't working, and whether there are lapses in logic or vagueness in the language. Is anything confusing? Not properly supported? Are some of the arguments less effective than others? What questions do the arguments evoke? What, in their opinion, is the meaning of the piece? By seeking this outside view-point, you will be able to embrace a reader-centred perspective of your work and this will help to articulate the difference between what you intend to say and what's actually on paper.

RELAX... There is no need to attack this task all in one go. I know how overwhelming that can feel so my advice is to work through the process in bite-sized chunks. Whether the piece is five pages or five hundred, wrap your head around the revision by breaking it up into manageable pieces. Work on one chapter, section, or scene at a time, and then step back and examine how these changes affect the overall piece. Pick a new focus for each round of revision.

Through this process, you can really think about tightening up on your language. "A sentence should contain no unnecessary words, a paragraph no unnecessary sentences, for the same reason that a drawing should have no unnecessary lines and a machine no unnecessary parts. This requires not that the writer make all sentences short or avoid all detail and treat subjects only in outline, but that every word tell." (Elements of Style, 4th ed, p.23)

There is a fantastic tool that will support you in cleaning up your grammar and ensuring you are writing in a grammatical sense: it is called *Grammarly*. You can install a free version of this on your computer from the website: www.-grammarly.com

The editing and revisions process is as simple as that. Don't overthink it. Allow yourself the headspace and time to consider the above questions to ensure you take advantage of any feedback that you receive.

YOUR FINAL MANUSCRIPT

$\mathcal{W}$e have made it... your final manuscript in all its glory! For this next part, what I want to cover is a few steps that you can take to ensure your book really is as good as you can make it. After the work that has gone in, you owe it to yourself and your book to get these final checks actioned.

The very first thing I recommend that you do is print out your manuscript, so you have it to hand. I know it's using ink and is probably a lot of pages to print off, but it's a really good idea to hold a printed copy of your first draft in your hands. When you read the words on paper, you are able to see things from a different perspective. See how the format differs on the version in your hand compared to the computer. As you go, take notes in longhand, which has been proven to force your brain to slow down and think about what you're doing and to process ideas more creatively.

Next, set it aside. Give yourself a complete break from your book for a day or two, even if you're in a big hurry to get it out the door, because I promise you'll be a much better editor of your own book if you look at it with fresh eyes. Now, some writers wait several weeks before they go back to their books, especially if they're writing novels. If you're trying to create a catalogue of books or you're trying to meet a specific deadline, you may not have the luxury of this much time. However, you should give yourself a little space between the first draft and your efforts to create a final manuscript. This may take two or three attempts.

The next step is to read the entire thing over one time. And when you do this, try to put yourself in the position of the reader who's ultimately going to read your book. Read the entire book, not with an editor's eye but with the reader's perspective in mind. For now, when you're doing this first read-through, don't worry about spelling and grammar, just read through it as if you were reading the book yourself. As you're reading, ask yourself these questions.

- Does it flow?
- Does it make sense?
- Is it repetitive?
- Am I bored by it?
- Does it sound too formal or too casual?
- Does it sound preachy or does it lack confidence?
- Are the chapters ordered properly?

- Did I leave out anything important?

After you've asked yourself these questions, you want to get somebody else to read it. And this is a good point in the process to ask someone who's your ideal reader to review the book. In fact, ask a few people who might be your ideal readers. Let them know exactly what you're looking for in the comments you want back from them. They don't need to edit for spelling and grammar, but you want them to answer the same questions as you did above.

Remember, people are always happy to offer constructive criticism and critiques, and these can be really useful. But also, pay attention to any positive comments or whether the book moved or inspired your readers. That's really great information for you. What you want to do next is cut and paste some of these comments from people into a document and save them onto a file so you can refer to it later when you're reconstructing and reviewing. You will find this super helpful later in the process.

With all of this new feedback to hand, you then want to handle any big reconstructions to your book first. Between the comments you get from other people and any ideas you've had in reading the first draft, you're going to have to take care of this restructuring process. It is the most difficult part of creating a second, third and final manuscript. I think it's really good to just go ahead and get that out of the way. You might want to do this with another outline altogether, or you can take your printed book copy and use arrows to show where you're going to move chunks of text. Then go back to your computer when you're ready and move around these chunks of text that you identified.

Now, you may discover that as you move this text around, some of the material you restructure needs a little bit of tweaking and rewriting. For example, you may need some different transition sentences to make the copy flow or you may need to change some of the material to fit better if you move it into a different chapter that has a different title.

Then you're going to want to rewrite the entire first draft – It won't take as long as it sounds: you are just getting everything back in order.

Once you've finished the major reconstructing, what you then want to do is go through the entire book to rewrite elements of it based on your notes and based on the ideas that you got from other people who read your book. You may or may not have rewritten the material you restructured, as I mentioned before. But even if you did, go through that one more time just to make sure it makes sense and you didn't miss anything as you were going through that reconstructing process.

As you read the entire book, tighten, tighten, and tighten everything up. Get rid of extraneous words, slash excess adverbs, clarify any ideas that seem kind of loose and sloppy. Take out any quotes, or jokes, or humour, or anything else that doesn't seem to work as well as you thought it did the first time around.

Next, you want to move on to review spelling, grammar and syntax. If you're not an expert at all of this, don't worry, that's why you can hire an editor. But you do want to do your best at reading through everything carefully one final time, just to make sure you're not missing anything that's glaringly obvious. And when you do this, you're going to save your editor time, but you're also going to save yourself a little money because they don't have to go back and make those corrections that could be obvious to you.

Finally, you want to avoid editing overkill. You may be the kind of a person who likes to reread your manuscript a dozen times and still you don't feel like it's quite right. And if you have that luxury of time, then go for it, that's fine. But it's not a good idea to spend so much time rewriting that you kind of lose time on other books that you could be writing.

Eventually, you're going to have to say, "Good enough is good enough," and go ahead and publish it. And then, over time, you'll continue to learn from your mistakes, and every book that you write will be an improvement on the last one. So, you need to know when to cut the cord and move on.

BOOK COVER DESIGN

*O*h, yes! We are finally here and I get so excited talking about your book cover design. The cover is personal to everyone and really brings your book to life. When you hold your book in your hand and see your name on it, it's that book cover that you are going to be looking at. It's the beautiful touch that makes your book complete and I know is an incredibly special part of the process for any author.

There are a few things that you need to know before you get started and I am going to take you through them one by one so you can get super clear when it comes to your cover.

Think like a reader, not like a writer

When it comes to cover images and text, it's really important that these can be clearly understood as thumbnails, which is how more books are being sold today.

If you cannot discern the image or read the text in the size it would be shown on one of the online bookstores, like Amazon, then the reader won't be able to, either.

Think of your cover as the key piece of the puzzle

Writing a book, to me, is like solving a mind-boggling jigsaw puzzle, blind-folded. After writing it, the final piece of this puzzle is to find the design that will get the attention of the customers you want. It is worthwhile asking for ideal client feedback because we want your cover to make your readers 'feel' something rather than just 'tell' them something.

Stick to genre expectations

When you browse the Amazon bestsellers in your genre, you should notice patterns in colour schemes, fonts, layout, and images. You want your cover to stand out by looking awesome, yet ensure it naturally fits into your genre. If you go against what readers of your genre expect to see, your book will end up in front of the wrong readers (and not sell). Once it's in front of the right readers, with a great cover, title, blurb, and reviews, it should get a lot more sales.

Shop for your cover on Amazon

As you shop on Amazon, keep your eye out for any book covers that stand out or that you find appealing. It can be helpful to look at the book covers you like and find inspiration, even if those covers are off topic or from another genre. When you find a book cover image you like on Amazon, just save the image to your desktop or to your book project management area. I personally have a file on my desk that is filled with covers I've seen when shopping or doing research that I loved for one reason or another.

Find inspiration on Pinterest

An awesome place for finding book cover ideas is Pinterest. You can browse boards and pins, then save the ones you like to your profile to refer to later. There are plenty of book cover boards you can browse to see which covers you're drawn to and serve as inspiration for your book's content, message, and genre.

So now let's think about how we can bring all of this together. One of the most important steps to your book cover is identifying if you're going to tackle this project yourself or hire a professional cover designer. Let me shine some light on these options for you.

If you want to design the cover yourself

I can recommend some of the best tools you can utilise and how you can use them with my own feedback for your reference.

Let's start with my personal favourite:

CANVA - This is a free design tool you can use with tons of

book cover templates for just about anything you'd want to design, including book covers for each genre. It's incredibly easy to use, but quite limited in what you can create.

DIY BOOK COVERS - This platform allows you to design your own book cover with free templates and tutorials based on the principles that work for bestselling books. It's a tool, a guide and a template system all in one.

ADOBE SUITE - If you have Photoshop, Illustrator or InDesign software already, you can learn how to use it to create book covers. It's quite a bit more advanced, but it does allow for much better more complex designs.

If you want to hire a professional book cover designer

So, let's look at outsourcing....

100 COVERS - This is a very affordable option for those who need a professional cover.

REEDSY - Here, you will find a marketplace for vetted book designers with high accomplishments in the industry. You're sure to find a fantastic cover designer or interior designer (formatter) with experience in your genre here.

99 DESIGNS - With this platform, you create a design contest by telling them what you're looking for, and you'll get lots of options in return. At the end of the week, you get to pick your favourite design. If you don't like any of the designs at the end, you get your money back – win-win!

Authors & Co recommended book cover designer

We are incredibly lucky to have a design and brand expert within our very own company, the incredible Tim Barber. Tim completes most of the covers for the authors who choose to publish with us on our signature programme so feel free to have a nosey on our website at some of the unique designs he has created. Please also bear in mind that some authors use their own brand designers so not all covers are his work.

Here is what Tim has to say about cover creation:

Experience

"I have worked on every genre of book you could imagine. From fantasy novels to edge of your seat thrillers, weight loss cookbooks to apocalyptic science fiction and chic-lit love stories to Victorian crime novels. This experience can help with your novel massively. No matter how original you feel your content is, and it could well be, you are still going to want a book cover that appeals to the masses. Your book's content can break all the rules, but your cover still has to show its genre and capture the attention of its intended audience, and that is where my experience will definitely help."

Great Design

"The most important thing is that you can be sure you will end up with a good book cover design. I'm experienced in

Adobe Photoshop and Adobe Indesign, and I have worked in the graphic design industry for years. Not only that, I have a huge passion for book cover design and book cover art, and it is this passion that drives me to go the extra mile. I will research your novel's genre, I will look for the latest book cover trends, I will brainstorm your story and I will put my heart and soul into the cover design. Whether it be paperback, ebook or hardback, fiction or non -fiction, I will create a design that will give your book a fantastic chance to get seen and read. After all, contrary to what your grandmother told you, we do all judge a book by its cover"

The Personal Touch

"Because I'm not a large corporation or an agency, you will be speaking to me and only me. Now, this may not seem that important to you, but what could be worse than the person you have told all your ideas not actually being the person designing your book cover? You will speak to me and only me and I will keep you up to date during the whole process. This is a much simpler and more efficient way of working and I feel it definitely results in a more enjoyable experience for an author and ultimately a better book cover design."

Bespoke Service

"Now, you may look through lots of cover designs and think to yourself that none of them match your book's content or that they aren't to your taste, and that is okay.

After all, what 'looks good' is subjective. That is why I offer a completely bespoke design service. The cover art that I design for you will be tailored to your book. The imagery will match the content and the typography will complement the design. Your book cover will not only be beautifully constructed, but it will fit your novel's genre and appeal to its intended audience."

Now we have looked at the various options for bringing your book cover to life, you may be interested to learn where you can source some beautiful copyright free images to use if you choose to do it yourself.

The stock images on these sites are free for you to use and adapt as long as you give the artist credit. If you use an image for your cover art, check the attribution guidelines to see if there are specific locations (such as back cover or title page) where artist credit should be given.

- Flickr
- Pixabay
- Pexels
- Free Images
- Unsplash

If none of these sparks your fancy, you can also source paid book cover images. Here are a few of the paid sites and memberships.

- Depositphotos
- Stock Unlimited
- Shutterstock

I hope the above has given you some great tools for you to consider when it comes to your book cover. The truth is, people do judge a book by its cover. If your book cover design doesn't follow these key guidelines, no matter how well it is written, it could be setting you up to fail.

So, make sure you can answer "Yes!" to all of these book cover design questions:

Does your cover send a clear message?

Did you stick to genre expectations?

Did you select a font that's proven to be great?

Did you use colours that complement and pop?

Did you choose a powerful picture that intrigues?

Does your cover make an impact in the small thumbnail size?

Did you brand your covers appropriately if you are writing a series?

Did you test your covers to see which is truly the best?

Implement these steps and you'll be well on your way to designing a book cover that's perfect for your market. A small point to remember before you start designing your book cover: do make sure that the dimensions of your book meet the market's requirements. Then, it's important to make sure you choose the right width to height ratio so that your book looks like it fits.

Enjoy this part of the book process, lovely: it will really bring your book to life!

ISBNS

*a*n ISBN (International Standard Book Number) is a 13-digit numeric code that serves as an internationally unique identifier for books. The barcode number holds lots of information regarding the book's publisher, title details, language, and edition. It helps customers identify and order the exact book they want to purchase. Libraries, book shops, distributors, online retailers, and wholesalers depend on this unique number to track sales, so it will be necessary to apply for an ISBN if you intend to sell to any of them. On the other hand, if you are purely publishing via Amazon, for example, an ISBN is not required whatsoever for an eBook on this platform and you can have a free one allocated for your paperback version.

Each version (ebook, hardcover, paperback, or audiobook) will require a separate ISBN, and in the following circumstances, it will become necessary to apply for a new ISBN:

- If you are making substantial textual changes that would qualify as a new edition
- If you are changing your publisher
- If you are changing your book title
- If the book is translated into another language.

If you intend on pursuing the traditional publishing route, your publisher will be your book's 'publisher of record'. However, if you are self-publishing, you have the option of using an ISBN assigned by your partnership publishing company or getting your own ISBN.

Here are the advantages to getting your own ISBN:

- You have total control over what is entered in your book's metadata—that being, the description and categories that will help libraries, shops, and readers globally discover your book and decide whether they want to purchase it. In today's digital world, your book's metadata can hugely impact its chances of being found and purchased by your target audience. This is really important to self-published authors, who most likely do not have the marketing and distribution capabilities of a traditional publisher.
- Any individual or organisation with specific orders or inquiries regarding your book will approach the publisher of record; you would rather this be you instead of your publishing service company.

Each country has an agency that issues ISBNs. Bowker is the official ISBN agency for the US, whereas authors in the UK can approach Neilson. Prices vary with quantity, so for example, a block of 1000 is far more cost effective than a block of 10 or a single ISBN. For a self-publishing author, buying a block of 10 makes more economic sense than buying just one or two for, say, the paperback and hard-cover versions, just in case you choose to make any of the above updates.

While the ISBN serves as a unique book identifier, retailers of physical books (paperback/hardback) use barcodes to manage their stock by reading the barcode at the time of purchase and sale. You can usually get a bar code from the agency that supplied you the ISBN.

So you have free and paid for options depending on how you want to publish, and they are absolutely required for paperback and hardback books.

TITLES, SUBTITLES & KEYWORDS

*T*he next part of the process is about keywords. It might sound like a boring bit, but knowing this stuff is going to give you a great advantage when it comes to getting your book out into the big wide world. As well as looking at the importance of keywords within your book, I also want to give you a step by step guide on how you too can carry out your own keyword research. This knowledge is imperative to your success. It doesn't stop there. We will also be looking at how to use this within KDP (Kindle Direct Publishing) when you upload your book, in line with utilising Amazon's very powerful search predictor. I intend to give you as much as I can on this as I know how powerful it can be. Bur first, I am going to be elementary and go straight into what the big deal is with keywords.

To start simply, 'keywords' are the words and phrases that internet users type into a search box of a search engine such as Google, YouTube and Amazon in order to find a match for what they are looking for. If you are an internet user, you probably do this on a regular basis yourself too.

Did you know that Amazon is one of the largest search platforms in the world along with Google and YouTube? As an author, this is exciting news! All platforms serve their very own purposes but in terms of the keyword search, it's pretty much the same. Like Google, Amazon tracks keywords, which are actually the search terms that potential buyers use when looking for a book or product. Amazon knows that single keywords and keyword phrases are very important, especially when it comes to their customers' product selection process.

Ssshhhhhh… Just like Google, Amazon keeps its actual search algorithm a secret. If you head over to Amazon, however, you will notice the strategic placement of the Amazon search bar. It's big, wide, white, and is centred at the top of every page for easy access. I know I never struggle to search for what I am looking for! It's in effect the centrepiece of the amazon.com experience.

Have you ever noticed that whenever you enter a keyword, Amazon's very sophisticated auto research predictor lists words and phrases to complete your search? These are the most commonly searched words and phrases that they have saved on their database. It's what people from around the world have predominantly searched for so its in essence guiding you to the answer it predicts you are looking for.

If you're not convinced yet about doing keyword research and the importance of keywords for publishing your books, then consider this. When you upload your book into KDP, Amazon invites you to leave up to seven keywords or key phrase strings, so that should tell you something there. They also allow you to use keywords in the title, subtitle and book description and this is where it can get really powerful.

Heading back to making a search on Amazon, I want you to now see how you can take advantage of their powerful auto-suggest box in the search bar. Let's say I am interested in the topic 'how to sleep better' or the general niche around sleep problems. As I start to type in 'how to sleep', even before I finish that phrase, Amazon automatically generates suggestions or similar types of keyword phrases. As an author, what you want to do here is start to collect some of these suggestions. My advice is to pop them onto a spreadsheet so you can start building your list of suggested keywords and phrases related to your niche and book topic. You want to follow this process again on YouTube, the world's third largest search engine, in exactly the same way. So, using my example above I would hop onto YouTube and type into the search bar 'How to sleep better' and you will see there are some other ideas in there too. These are phrases that are saved in YouTube's search database. Then, go and do the same on Google, the world's largest search engine.

The magic of using search engines to generate specific

keywords and phrases for you doesn't need to stop there. If you slightly tweak your search, even more suggestions will come up for you to add to your spreadsheet.

Just before we dive a little deeper into all of this with the focus on Google, I want to remind you of the kind of goals we are after here. These keywords and phrases will become the foundations for your book title, subtitle, description, etc. and will support your book to become more visible to potential buyers interested in your niche and topic. We can also use these to reference some of the potential customers' problems and their questions and get a real feel for the type of language people use. With this, we hear the pain in that language. If they can find the solution to their pain in your book with your book title, description and/or subtitle, then you can really engage people to read further.

Let's take a further look.

When people go to a search engine or a search box on Amazon, they are trying to find something. A lot of times they are trying to find an answer to a problem or a question that they need the answer to. You do this regularly yourself, right?

I want to let you know about an invaluable tool that is going to help you discover even more keywords and phrases. It's called Google's Keyword Planner. If you head over to google.com and enter the words 'Keyword planner' the first item that will pop up is their very own tool. This is a super powerful tool and one I would recommend you take full advantage of when it comes to keyword searches for your very own book.

So, as you can see, the keyword element is going to give you a great advantage when it comes to getting your book seen by the right people. It really forms the foundations of your title, subtitle and book description, which is where we are heading next.

YOUR BOOK DESCRIPTION

*W*e're now moving on to one of the most important marketing materials for your book, the description. The book description is visible on the back cover (for paperbacks) or the inside flap copy (for hardbacks) and right below the price (on Amazon). As one of the most influential factors which cause people to actually read your book or not, it's vital that you take the time to consider and apply every key element that I am going to walk you through for your own description.

I want to give you some perspective on the power of your description in relation to your sales. There are so many examples of how book descriptions have led to huge changes in sales, that it's incredible authors don't spend more time getting it right. One of my favourite examples of this is Mark Edwards' book, Killing Cupid. Despite a great cover and a number of good reviews, it wasn't selling as many copies as it should have been. He dove into the competition, analysed their descriptions, and completely revamped his description. Sales doubled... within an hour. This isn't uncommon. In many cases, the description is the factor that solidifies in the reader's mind whether the book is for them or not. If you get it this bit right, the purchase is almost automatic. If you get it wrong, you will probably lose the sale there and then.

Don't worry, you are in safe hands. I am going to walk you through some key elements to help you cultivate your powerful book description.

Realise it's an Ad, not a summary

It's really important here to not think about your book as a synopsis, but instead view it as an advertisement. It is not meant to summarise your book. It is designed to make people want to read your book and our main objective is for them to take action and buy it. So many authors want to make this too long by putting everything about their book in this section. Resist that urge. Remember, when you are searching on Amazon, what you are looking for in a random book description is a reason to read the book.

So how can we give people a reason to buy it? You state the problem or question your book addresses, you show that you solve or answer it, but leave a small key piece out. This piques the interest of the reader and leaves them wanting more.

Great first line

Grab them in the first sentence. If that isn't quite right – or worse, if it's wrong – you can lose the reader immediately, and then it doesn't matter what the rest of the description says. People are always looking for a reason to move on to the next thing. Don't give it to them. Make the first sentence something that intrigues or encourages them to read the rest of the description.

Make it personal and relevant

It's important to make the description personal here, clearly explaining why someone interested in the problem being solved needs to read it. Done right, you will create an emotional connection with your potential reader by describing how the book will make them feel after reading it. Or even better, the transformation the reader will get out of reading your book.

For example, will it make them happy or rich? Will it help them lose weight or have more friends? What else? Be clear about the benefits, don't insinuate them. You are making a promise and selling a result to the reader, not a process (even though your book is the process).

Don't hide the what or the how

Explain exactly what the book is about, in crystal clear terms. Do not make the reader struggle to understand what your point is, or how you get the reader there. For some books, it's not enough to write a compelling ad with important keywords; sometimes you need to give readers a sense of where this book is going and how it gets there. This is especially true for prescriptive books (how-to, self-help, motivational, etc.). People like to understand the "how" as well as the "what," especially if it's something new or novel (that being said, make sure to leave just enough mystery to make them buy the book).

Use compelling wording

It's not enough to be accurate, you need to use high traffic keywords that increase the likelihood your book will get picked up in the search.

Bullet points are OK

If it makes sense for what you're trying to convey, use bullet points to list out the information. They are an effective visual tool that makes your description scannable and easily digestible.

Do use beneficial referencing

Don't compare with other books but DO use what benefits the book does have. If there is an impressive fact to mention (e.g. NYT Bestseller), that will be bolded in the first sentence. Or if there is something 'stand-out' about you or your book, that can go in the book description, something like, "From the author of (insert well known bestselling book)" or perhaps "From the award-winning" etc.

If you're struggling, get help

I can't tell you how many amazing authors I've had come to me utterly confuzzled because they couldn't write their own book description. This is normal. The reality is that the author is often not the best person to write their own book description. They're too close to the material and too emotionally invested. If this is the case, I recommend going to a professional editor or even better – a professional copywriter for assistance.

So, with the tips covered, let's take a look at what this logistically looks like. On average, the Amazon bestsellers have descriptions that are about one hundred and fifty to two hundred and fifty words long. Not so daunting, right? With this, most descriptions are broken up into two paragraphs, some are kept at one and some run to three. So, look at what your description needs and run with what works for you.

When it comes to how you need to write, keep it simple. Short, clear sentences are far more powerful. You don't want anyone to struggle to comprehend what you're trying to convey because you've strung too many ideas together in one long sentence.

Write as a publisher, not the author: this will probably be obvious to you, but the book description should always be in a third person objective voice, and never your author voice.

Hopefully, this has given you a really clear perspective into your book description. Remember, it can make or break whether someone decides to read your book so do give it the time and due diligence it deserves.

A 'WOW' AMAZON AUTHOR PROFILE

*O*nce you have published you book, the next step is to set up your Amazon Author Central account. This platform will allow you to build an author profile whilst helping you track book sales, see and respond to reviews, interact with your audience, fix issues with your listings and add editorial reviews. Any author with a book listed for sale on Amazon can sign up for an Amazon Author Central account and will find it absolutely invaluable.

Once you've set up your Author Central account, you'll be able to get started on an Amazon Author Page – which will be your new or existing readers' go-to source for any information they could ever want to know about you and your work. It is ultimately where people will head to read your author bio, see or buy your books, find links to your site or social platforms and learn more about you.

Let's say, for example, that a reader loved your first book and is interested in buying your second. Or that they've read your work and want to know more about your personal or professional background. Your Amazon Author Page acts as a one stop shop for them to get all of this done, while showcasing a complete library of your products.

Here's what you should include on yours in order to really make it work for you:

1. Biography and social media links

Tell your audience about yourself! While a CV tells prospective employers about your professional history, this is your chance to highlight your achievements in life and as an author to your prospective readers. You'll be able to list all of your books and use your bio area as a means to showcase your personal and professional achievements, projects, hobbies and any other information that your readers would find interesting. This is also where you can list your social media, website and blog links. Make sure to hyperlink them in the text so that anybody reading can simply click through.

2. Professional author photos and relevant videos

Readers like see the person behind the book. It's worth noting that you can branch out and get creative with the author photos you add to your page. Of course, it's best to include at least one professional author shot – but many writers also showcase a variety of personal photos that relate to the content they publish. If you're an artist for example, upload photos of yourself with your artwork or at a gallery receiving recognition for the work you've done and so on. If you'd like to step it up a notch, add a few videos to your profile. Amazon Author Pages support up to eight videos that are a maximum of ten minutes in length. Showcase yourself speaking at an exhibition or teaching your audience DIY art techniques, or put together a video compilation of your best work. The opportunities are endless.

3. A library of your books

If a reader has devoted the time and energy to looking up your Amazon Author page, chances are he or she is interested in finding out about the other books you've written. Take the opportunity to showcase all your work in a digital library format and be sure to keep this section updated whenever you publish new products. When an Amazon user lands on your page based on a keyword search, imagine their delight (and your heightened opportunity to make sales) when they realise that you've written an entire book series about, let's say, "becoming a marketing guru". If the entire series hadn't been listed here, they likely would never have stumbled upon it.

4. Editorial reviews

Most of us are familiar with Amazon's generic review section, but what many authors overlook is its incredibly valuable editorial reviews section. This is where you can share up to five professional testimonials that other industry leaders within your niche or valuable contacts of yours have made about your book(s). Your editorial reviews are a prime channel through which to easily boost your credibility and position yourself as an authority on the subject you're writing about.

5. A convenient feed to your blog posts

What better way to increase traffic to your blog than by linking it to your Amazon Author Page? Whether you've just started blogging, are hoping to get more hits on your site or already receive thousands of visits per month, there's no downside to linking your feed to your account. Whenever you upload a new blog post, it'll automatically update on your Amazon Author Page – allowing users to visit your site with one simple, effortless click.

6. Follow button

Typically, the Follow button on your page is already activated. This will allow Amazon users to subscribe to your updates and be notified whenever you publish a new book or make important announcements via your Author Page.

Don't overlook international author pages. Now that you've gone through the motions of updating and optimising your Author Page, there's one last step to consider. Given that Amazon is broken down into international markets, you could be missing out on lots of sales if you choose to only set yourself up on one site. Although it's time consuming, consider expanding your reach by creating an Amazon Author Page within the multiple Amazon markets that exist globally today.

7

LAUNCHING WITH LOVE

YOUR BOOK MARKETING TIMELINE

*H*ere comes the 70% - Yes, you read that correctly. Writing and publishing your book is around thirty percent of the whole picture. The overall success of your book is weighted in more like 70% of the marketing.

I suggest that right away you create a book marketing calendar to keep you focused and on track with your marketing activities in the months leading up to, and extending beyond, your book launch. This marketing timeline includes example marketing activities and when in the process you might want to focus on them. But you know your book and market better than anyone else (or at least you should), so adapt things where necessary. Re-schedule things, add things to it, ignore things you don't plan to use, and make it your own.

Whilst you are writing

- Set up your author website.
- Set up your social media profiles if you don't already have them.
- Start building your reputation as an authority on your topic.
- Post to your author blog regularly.
- Create an editorial calendar filled with content ideas to take you through at least one month after your book release.
- Start actively building your social networks and building relationships with friends or followers.

4-6 months before you launch

- Set up an account with an email marketing service and start building your list.
- Send occasional emails to your list (a couple of times a month is often enough).
- Build a preliminary list of influencers or target reviewers.
- Build a list of blogs, websites, and other publications or media outlets you'd like to appear in during your launch publicity.
- Build a media list for PR distribution.

3 months before you launch

- Create a marketing calendar to help you stay on top

of appearances, guest blog posts, interview dates, etc.

- Start writing guest blog posts early (as soon as you get confirmation from hosts) so that you don't become overwhelmed later on.
- Have a book trailer created.
- Have your author headshot taken. Add it to your website and all social media profiles. You're looking to build a consistent image.
- Start to build a launch team to help support your launch when the time comes.

1-2 months before you launch

- Add a sales page for your book to your website or blog. You can keep this a secret until launch day unless you're accepting pre-orders.
- Create your media kit (Q&As, professional author photos and book cover images, your launch press release, etc.).
- Write your launch day press release.
- Contact potential reviewers and send advanced copies.
- Pre-write some social media updates in advance promoting your book (include excerpts to unique articles related to your book).
- Release your book trailer.
- Plan and run a pre-launch contest.

1 week before you launch

- Schedule your pre-written social media content.
- Confirm any upcoming guest slots, interviews, live appearances, etc.
- Track comments on any guest blog posts or online interviews that have gone live and take the time to respond.
- Post an excerpt of your book or even the first chapter, to get your audience excited about seeing the rest of your book.
- Prepare material for your author pages on key websites (Amazon, Goodreads, etc.).
- Prepare your launch team with what you would like them to do/share.

The day of the launch

- Make sure your book information is showing correctly on distribution sites.
- Announce your book launch on your blog or author profile.
- Announce your book launch via social networks and take the time to thank and respond to others who share your news.
- Send out your launch day press release.
- Add "available now" links to everywhere that is relevant.
- Add a link to your book's sales page to your email

signature and any relevant forum signatures.

- Send out an email newsletter to your mailing list with a link to buy your book.
- Hold a launch party or book release/signing event if you want to.

1-3 months post-launch

- Send "thank you" notes, emails, cards, or gifts to people who helped you promote your book.
- Continue to seek reviews for your book.
- Continue posting to your blog to keep regular readers engaged. End each post with a call to action related to your book.
- Continue updating your social media accounts.
- Continue to work on your publicity (online or in-person).
- If you've received a great review or testimonial, ask the reviewer if you can share them in whole or on your platforms.
- Plan a contest to create fresh interest around your book.
- Submit your book for any appropriate awards.

Now that we have gone through ALL of that, promise me you won't freak out. I know it seems a lot, (and it is) but that 70% will ensure your book's overall success.

It's worth it!

POWER IN NUMBERS

*W*hen I work with new authors, one of the first 'to do list' tasks I assign is to build a list of people you want in your launch team. This is important whether you already have a platform or not, because you might be surprised at how many people you know who can help support your book and your overall goal.

You can begin to build your launch team months ahead of your book launch. In fact, you should make it a priority to start forming these relationships now so you know who you can ask for support when your book is published.

How Can Your Launch Team Members Help?

- Beta Reader Support: To provide you with valuable feedback and a review when you launch.
- Book Sales: Purchase copies of your book during

your launch campaign and share your posts and announcements with their own audiences.

- Bulk Sales: Buy copies of your book in bulk to distribute within their own network/at their own events.
- Endorsements: Well-known authors, influencers or celebrities can provide testimonials for your book cover or contribute a foreword.
- Industry Promotion: Recommend your book in an industry specific blog, newsletter, or magazine.
- Reviews: Post reviews on Amazon, Goodreads and directly for your website.
- Social Media: Share book promotion messages across social media platforms.
- Podcasts: Feature you on an industry podcast, summit or webinar.
- Speaking Opportunities: Invite you to/recommend you to speak at a meeting, event or conference.
- Sponsorship: Contribute to your book project or launch by donating funds or in-kind items, such as printing services or banners/balloons, in exchange for promotion.
- Connections and Warm Introductions: In addition to asking your launch tribe for the above support, you can also ask them, *"Who do you know who can help?"* You'll never know if you don't ask!

How to Build Your List of Launch Team Supporters

Spend some quiet time brainstorming a list of people you can contact and ask for support. Create spreadsheets to keep track and organise them based on the opportunities listed above.

Consider the following people:

- Friends and family – These shouldn't be your main review sources because you want your book reviews to come from 'ideal' readers. However, your closest family and friends may be able to connect you with people who can help you accomplish your goals whilst being your biggest cheerleaders.
- Social media groups – If you participate in groups that reach your target readers, ask the group owner if you can share book announcements or invite beta readers from the group. Facebook groups that focus on your niche can be a fantastic place to build your readership.
- Fellow authors – Authors who have a large platform can have a big impact on book sales simply by recommending your book to their own tribe via social media or their email list.
- Influencers – This includes bloggers, podcast hosts, YouTubers, and social media stars.
- Current and past clients – If someone has really enjoyed working with you, they will likely be happy to support your new book launch.

- Past readers – Readers who loved your previous book(s) could certainly be interested in your next one!
- Social media followers – This is one of the many reasons why authors should build a social media following of loyal fans.
- Media professionals – Build a list of journalists, editors and producers who are either local or cover topics related to your book.
- Email list subscribers – If you're not yet building an email list, you should be. This is hands down one of the best marketing tools you can have. (More on this next!)

Once you have compiled your lists, your next step is to start reaching out. Some people on your list should be contacted individually, while others can be contacted in groups.

People who know you WANT to support you. Sometimes all you have to do is ask.

EMAIL MARKETING

*L*et's talk about the importance of email marketing. Despite the rise of social media and unsolicited spam, email still remains one of the most effective ways to nurture potential readers and turn them into customers. Starting your email list sooner rather than later will give you a huge advantage when it comes to your launch.

Although there are a ton of reasons you should make email marketing one of your top priorities, here are the three main ones...

- Email is an incredible communication channel. Around 90% of consumers check their email on a daily basis.
- You own your list. On any social media platform, your account (with all your followers) could be

suspended or deleted at any time, for any reason, without notice. However, you own your email list. No one can take those contacts away from you.

- Email converts well when nurtured. The average order value of an email is at still at least three times higher than that of social media.

Where to start...

Choose an email provider that is right for you. There are so many options ranging from free to much more expensive depending on how techy and sophisticated you want to go. I personally started out with Mailchimp's free plan and now use one of Active Campaigns paid options. It's important that unless you are outsourcing this area of your marketing, that you choose something that feels nice and simple for you to navigate.

When it comes to growing your email list

What most people do when they want to build an email list is to put an 'opt-in' form on their website and hope that people sign up. Unfortunately, this strategy usually doesn't work very well to get people excited about your book. It actually works better when you have a digital version of your book that you could offer them in exchange. To grow your email list in time for your book launch, you need to attract people with a compelling offer. You need what's called a lead magnet.

A lead magnet is something amazing that you give away

for free in exchange for an email address. This doesn't have to cost you a penny to create– most lead magnets are digital materials like PDFs, MP3 audio files, or videos that you can create yourself at minimal or no cost. It can be anything you want, so long as it provides value for free. Think about what would attract your ideal reader.

Some popular lead magnet examples are...

- An eBook (So you can use your book or at least some of your book afterwards)
- Tips or resources
- A case study
- A free webinar

The possibilities are endless!

What makes a good lead magnet?

- It needs to be easily consumed – Lead magnets are only effective when the audience uses them, so if you overwhelm your audience by delivering a 250 page document, you probably won't gain the traction you were hoping for. Keep it simple.
- It's action-driven – Lead magnets work well when they provide useful information that your audience can apply quickly.
- It creates a noticeable difference – People continue to buy products and services if they work. Your lead magnet will become successful if it's valuable.

- It's relevant – If you've done your homework about your ideal readers, you'll have no trouble coming up with a lead magnet that solves a problem for them.
- It's instant – People love instant downloads, so give it to them right there and then.

Now that you know what a lead magnet is and how to create a highly effective one, you'll need to create your opt-in form that converts for you. The purpose of your opt-in form is to convey the benefits of your lead magnet, so that your website visitors or social media followers subscribe to your email list in exchange for getting the lead magnet.

(Before we go any further, although it might be needless to say, your opt-in and way that you store data all need to be GDPR compliant.)

To create an opt-in form that converts, it needs to have the following components:

- An enticing headline – Make sure your headline clearly describes the promise/value of your lead magnet.
- A helpful description – Keep it brief, clear and to the point.
- An attractive visual – Include an image of the lead magnet if you can (e.g. a mock-up of your freebie). Or a photo of a happy person looking towards the opt-in form is a great way to boost conversions.

- A simple form – Don't try to ask for more than a first name and email address. Asking for too much information will kill your conversions because people just can't be bothered.
- A striking subscribe button – Make sure to use a contrasting colour for your subscribe button, so that it really pops out on the page. Also use copy that compels people to click right away (e.g. "Send me the 5 steps!").

Improving Your Email Open Rates

This section is important because even with all the hard work you've done to grow your email list, you won't benefit from any of it unless your emails actually get opened. And we particularly want all of your book launch emails opened! There are several factors which play a role in whether your emails get opened so take the following into consideration.

Avoid Spam Filters

The first and most obvious problem is when your email gets sent to the subscriber's spam folder. But since you've already obtained permission to send emails, and you've chosen a reputable email service provider, you're off to a better start than those who haven't.

Just make sure all recipients have opted in to receiving your emails and show them how to whitelist your emails and add you to their address book. Try and avoid the excessive use of "salesy" language (these are spam trigger words like "buy", "clearance", "discount", or "cash") and don't use deceptive subject lines. You also need to include a visible and simple unsubscribe option.

Remove Inactive Subscribers to Keep Your List Fresh

It's important to email your subscribers on a consistent basis, so your list doesn't go stale. That being said, over time, email subscribers can still go stale. Some of your fans may have changed email accounts, or maybe they just aren't interested in you/your brand anymore. Check in with your subscribers every once in a while to ask if they would like to update their information and their preferences. This way, they are reminded that they can take control of how they want to engage with you.

Make Your Subject Line Stand Out

When it comes to email open rates, it's your subject line that will normally determine whether your email gets opened or binned. Your job is to make sure that your subject lines are intriguing enough to open and entice curiosity, without trying to be too clever. You want to make them curious enough to open your email, but without being so cryptic that the subscriber hasn't a clue as to what you're talking about. Also, you may want to insert numbers. There is something about numbers that gets people's attention.

Write Amazing Content, Every Time

You may be thinking that when a subscriber opens your

email, you've essentially won the battle. However, the actual content of your email also plays an important role in your open rate. Here's why: if your subscribers are happy with your content, they are more likely to open your emails in the future. They may even begin to eagerly anticipate your emails. However, if a subscriber is disappointed or maybe even annoyed with what they got in your email, they probably aren't going to open your emails again, and they may even unsubscribe.

So how do you make sure you get your email content right? The key is to make sure that you aren't sending emails just to send emails. Every single time you email your list, you need to deliver something of real value and relevance. The higher the value of the emails you write, the more loyal your subscribers will become, and your open rates will increase.

Putting all of this into practice during the build up to your book launch should ensure you are both growing your audience, nurturing them and getting them excited for the arrival of your masterpiece.

AN ALLURING BOOK TRAILER

*W*herever you look online, you can see videos being used, shared and re-shared. Video for marketing is KING.

Video content has become more of a necessity than just an alternative to other marketing methods, and that needs to be taken into consideration for your book launch. While beautiful and compelling long-form prose is essential to bring your book to life, it can no longer be your primary method of promoting it online. There's just so much content out there vying for your potential reader's attention.

What can you do then?

Well, just as the subtitle has suggested, book trailers have gained more and more attraction as a powerful piece in any promotional campaign for a new book. However, as great as an excellent book trailer can be to help get your new non-fiction book out into the limelight, a bad one can easily make people actively avoid it!

Why some book trailers fail

To be a writer you need to be intimately familiar with story-telling. Yet it's not difficult to do a quick YouTube search and find tons of book trailers that are poorly put together: image slideshows with no storyline whatsoever. Just like adverts for a new film, trailers are meant to be narrative instruments. This means that all those other vital story-telling concepts that apply to other mediums should be accounted for in your book trailer as well.

Trailers have to tell a story and do so as they convey your book's message, tone, style, and intent – as subtly or as overtly as your work intends. Most importantly, this all needs to be captured in just a few seconds.

The Hook

Just as you slaved away for days on end tweaking and polishing your book's first few lines to make sure they captured any eager eyes that glanced at them, you need to strive to do the same with your trailer's opening moments. Don't forget what you are going up against: an endless stream of posts, competing for attention.

Most of these watchers will decide whether to engage or not with your content within the first three seconds, so the beginning of your trailer is paramount. Find a sequence, sentence or opening capable of hooking your viewers to keep them glued.

The Premise

Your trailer should be able to communicate the basic premise of your book, without giving everything away. Just make sure you give out enough information for anyone watching to *"get"* what your book's about, while you fight the urge to reveal more than absolutely necessary to get them to the point where they want to know more.

The Characters

For non-fiction, the author should take the place of the main character in a trailer (*much in the way that documentary trailers do,*) providing something that the viewers can emotionally connect with and relate to.

The Music

Sound is another vital piece necessary to make a good book trailer: the music will determine both impact and emotion. Choosing the wrong piece of music can kill the mood you are trying to go for, which in turn can portray your book incorrectly. If you don't feel confident making this choice for your book, have a look through a few film trailers that may have a similar theme to your book and use the same musical principles in yours.

The Script

A script is an instrument that helps you guarantee that the whole thing *works*.

Strive to create a cohesive script for your trailer, one that supports the narrative and marketing goals you want it to achieve. When you're working on your trailer script, this is also an ideal format to start making annotations to guide other elements that will become relevant later, like visuals, imagery, animations, etc.

The Storyboard

Think of the storyboard of your trailer as being very similar to your book's outline. A storyboard is there to help make sure everything you started to set up in the script actually fits together in a more visual format. It has to take the viewer from point A to point B precisely the way you want it to. The way I designed my own was to think about all the important and emotional points in an author's journey, and to capture each one of them in way that makes the audience want to live the experience for themselves. Storyboards matter because they let you get a clear view of how all the significant elements of your trailer will come together and how these elements interplay before you have to invest even more time and money bringing the whole project into reality.

Finishing a book is such a full on and challenging project

for most authors that it's easy to feel overwhelmed once you are faced by the equally intimidating task of advertising it and letting people know about it. Yet, having a brilliant book trailer doing the rounds online showcasing your work, to strangers and followers alike, in a compelling and exciting way can make all the difference in the world towards achieving your goal.

PODCASTS

*I*t is a fact that podcasts drive higher conversion rates for book sales. Being able to listen to someone on a podcast can form a much more personal relationship than just reading an article they wrote. It's also more difficult to skim through a podcast in the way you can skim a blog and so they're going to hear the full story behind you and your book, not just the headlines.

Podcasts are more time efficient

It's also a much more leveraged use of scarce marketing time for an author. If you're focused on growing your audience, writing articles for other sites can be time consuming. A good article usually takes at least five hours to write and edit, and a great long article can take at least ten hours. An hour-long podcast, on the other hand, only takes, well, an hour. If you add on two more hours (one for research and one for prep), it's still only three hours vs ten.

Author, speaker and consultant Dorie Clark did over 150 podcast appearances in 2015, the year that "Stand Out" was released, and also said it was her number 1 channel for driving book sales. I listened to some of these podcasts at the time and couldn't wait to get my hands on her book!

It's a distribution channel which is rapidly growing, highly converting and requires less time and resources than others that are already proven to be profitable.

But wait, there's more

While the immediate benefits are worth it alone, another long-term benefit is the boost to your SEO. The podcast host will most likely have a show page already set up to link to your website, meaning that you'll have a diversified back-link profile from an authoritative source in your industry.

I haven't even mentioned the number one long-term benefit, which is that it's a great way to build relationships with influencers in your industry. Just as people hearing your voice lets you build a deeper relationship with the audience, talking on the phone for an hour lets you build a deeper relationship with the host. Short of meeting in person, hosting a podcast and bringing people on or appearing on someone else's podcast is the best way to get to know people. You get to talk for an hour in a way that mutually benefits both of you. The host gets a valuable piece of content to share with their audience and you get exposure to a new audience!

So how do you get featured on podcasts to support your book launch?

Build a list of podcast targets

The first thing you need to do is to figure out which podcasts would be a good fit. Use the following method to build a spreadsheet of targets:

Step 1: Do you know anyone that has a podcast? A friend of a friend? Introductions will convert much better than reaching out cold. Once you've been on a few podcasts, it gets easier to be on others because you're already vetted and tested as a podcast guest.

Step 2: Look for podcasts which have featured authors from a similar genre – who is an authority in your space that is a few years ahead of where you are right now? Make a list of five to ten people in your field and search their names on iTunes. The podcasts they've appeared on have a track record of having guests very similar to you! That's a positive sign that they would be willing to have you on too.

Step 3: Look for relevant New and Noteworthy Podcasts in iTunes – podcasts that are in the new and noteworthy categories have two very promising attributes:

They're new and so they NEED more guests to put out more episodes – and If they got into New and Noteworthy then they are probably good marketers which bodes well for the future success of their show and your interview. If you appear on one of the initial episodes, when people download their entire back catalogue four years into the future, they'll listen to your episode.

Step 4: Go to Amazon and see which authors have books on your topic. Authors tend to do a lot of podcasts, so you can search out authors who have books on similar topics to yours and use step 2 again to see what podcasts they've been on by searching their name on iTunes.

Prioritise the list

When you have a healthy list of options in your spreadsheet, prioritise it.

Step 1: Eliminate – first let's get rid of all the people that won't help you grow your numbers. Here are characteristics of a good outreach target. If a podcast doesn't match these, remove them for now:

- Have published an episode recently and appear to be continuing to do so regularly (weekly / monthly).
- Good brand match – get rid of anything which doesn't fit your values.
- They do interviews – some podcasts are solo podcasts where the podcaster gives their opinion on a topic or reads quotes. Make sure they actually have had guests on in the past!

Step 2: Prioritise

URL

Email address (If you can't find their email, add the contact page URL)

Twitter Handle

Once a podcast show/host looks like a good match, fill out a spreadsheet with all the following information about them:

Potential reach of their podcast – how popular is their podcast? It's very hard to know a podcast reach, even for podcasters themselves, and a lot don't share their numbers. I make an estimated guess based on how many Twitter followers they have:

H = Huge = 100k+ Followers

L = Large = 10K+ Followers

M = Medium = 1k+ Followers

S = Starting out = fewer than 1k Followers

Where you found them – make notes about how you found them to use when you reach out. Did they have an author similar to you on their podcast? Do you have a friend or connection in common that you can ask for an introduction?

Before getting in touch, read their About page – what do they have in common with you that could be a personal note? You may also want to listen to a popular episode of their podcast just to get a feel.

Come up with an angle to email them – one of the hardest

things podcasts have to do is figure out the angle of each show. How will they make this guest uniquely interesting and compelling to their audience? I know podcasters that spend a day or more preparing for each interview. If you do this work for them and explain why you can deliver a ton of value to their audience, they're much more likely to have you on.

Make a list of topics you can speak about. Here are the ones I focus on:

- Publishing
- Marketing
- Entrepreneurship
- Business with Babies

It's also a great idea to make a podcast bio that you can send across with your email. This will include not only your specialist topics above, but anything else you feel is relevant that may help "sell" you to the host.

Here is an example of the sort of email that you could send:

YOUR STORY STARTS HERE

Hey /name,

My name is.......... I have just published my first book,........... It's currently a best selling book in (name category) on Amazon. It sold over a thousand copies in the first month it was available and received some lovely endorsements including .... who was kind enough to include a two page review of the book in her magazine.

I'm contacting you because I think the book would be interesting for your audience and I'm hoping you would be interested in having me as a guest on your podcast. The book provides an overview of .... If you're interested in having me on, I've provided some information on the book below and would be happy to send you a copy. If not, no worries whatsoever and thanks for taking the time to put out your podcast.

Best Wishes, [Name]

QUICK BOOK SUMMARY TITLE:
ONE SENTENCE SUMMARY:
IT'S DIFFERENT THAN OTHER BOOKS ON
THE SUBJECT BECAUSE:
BOOK LINK HERE TO PDF:

Confirm the time

Once someone says yes, you want to get a time confirmed

to record right away. Again, think about making it easy for them.

Interview Techniques

Getting on podcasts is great, but it's only part of the battle. If you want podcasts to be an effective marketing channel, you need to deliver a brilliant interview.

- Become a great storyteller – Every answer you give should have an impactful story. People learn not through facts and stats, but through stories, analogies and metaphors. Think how you can tell a story or give an example that will answer any question they ask.
- Speak clearly and slowly – When you find yourself going too fast, think about lowering the pitch of voice. If you lower your voice, it will automatically slow you down.
- Speak Decisively – Don't say "Umm" or "So" or "Kind of" or stutter/repeat yourself. If you don't know what to say, just be silent then speak when you've composed your thoughts.
- Set up a custom landing page for their audience with freebies – Whatever lead magnet you are using on your website, set it up as a freebie and offer it to their audience using an easy to remember URL link. (Just make sure it's ok with the host that you do this.)

Follow up

Last but not least, thank the host again for having you on and ask if they know anyone else that would be interested. If you've done all the steps above, you're probably one of the better guests they've had. Since they're a podcaster, they probably know other podcasters who might be interested.

REVIEWS

*C*an you believe we are already thinking about reviews? The time will come around quickly, that I can promise you.

One of the most frequent questions I get when it comes to asking for book reviews is, is it ethical? Is it ethical to ask people to leave a review for your book? If you're approaching friends and family who haven't even read your book (or random people on the internet who also haven't read your book) and are asking them to leave what could only be a vague remark with a 5-star rating, then yes, I believe that is unethical. However, if you are asking people to read your book and then share an honest review, then that is ethical and a great benefit to you.

The key here is to ask for truthful reviews. When you reach out to your reviewers, make this very clear, and try to be open to negative reviews, if they were their honest thoughts. If you have committed to writing the very best manuscript you can, and you have engaged an awesome team to turn it into the best possible book it can be, this shouldn't be an issue. Even if there are a couple of people who don't appreciate you or your content, the good reviews will balance them out.

Is it worth it?

When we're looking for new products, choosing the best hotels and restaurants, searching for a holiday and even shopping for books, we all look at reviews and ratings. A product that has a good number of positive reviews and an average rating of 4-5 stars looks like a better deal. It looks like it will deliver on its promises. In the case of a non-fiction, how-to book, it looks like it actually teaches readers what it says it will teach them. This is especially true if we're comparing two similar books – if one has tens or hundreds of 5- star reviews and in-depth feedback, while another has no or few reviews (or worse, an average rating of only 1-3 stars), which would you choose?

Reviews also give you a great reason to continue talking about your book. Every time a great review comes in, you have something new to share on social media and with your email list. And if you've built a genuine relationship with your fans and followers, they will be genuinely excited on your behalf, which leads to likes, comments, and click throughs to your book's listing on Amazon. When you share your good reviews on social media or with your list, not only does it remind your followers that your book exists, it reminds them to visit Amazon.

Some reviewers have other channels where they publish their reviews – on their blogs, on Goodreads, on book review sites where they are members, all of which helps your book get in front of more people.

How do you do it?

1. Ask your beta readers

As discussed earlier, a great way to ensure you write the best book you can is to enlist a team of beta readers in the publishing process. Beta readers are simply your 'trial' readers who read your book before it is published to give you feedback on how you can improve your book, or what you may need to include/exclude. If they like it, why not take the opportunity to ask for a review at the same time?

2. Reach out to Amazon reviewers

Beta readers are wonderful, but if you don't have time to engage beta readers in your publishing journey (or if they don't get around to leaving a review), where else should you look?

Amazon.

Amazon has hundreds of millions of users, who have collectively left hundreds of millions of reviews for books and other purchases. When it comes to those reviews, other shoppers can vote on whether they found the review helpful (a thumbs up underneath), which then contributes to the ranking of the reviewer themselves on Amazon. If you look at Amazon's top rated reviewers, you'll find that not only have they reviewed a ton of products, but their reviews tend to be balanced and go into a lot of depth, which is why they have so many 'helpful' votes.

Why should this matter to you?

Amazon gives you easy access to reviewers who not only have the ability to read your book and provide a review pretty quickly, but who may put a lot of thought and energy into your review to ensure it is of great value. This makes the review more useful to your potential readers and (in the case of positive 4-5* reviews) a more powerful endorsement for your book.

3. Find relevant book reviewers

I've found the best way to find reviewers is to search out people who have already reviewed books like the one that you are writing. After all, this shows that they have an interest in your genre, which means they are more likely to read and then review your book.

Keep in mind that not everyone will respond to you, not everyone will agree to leave you a review, and some of those who do agree to read and review your book might not get around to it, so always aim for a minimum of fifty names on your list. You can compile a new list every few months, as more books like yours are released, and when more reviews have been added to the old ones. Create a spreadsheet with the reviewers' details, the book they reviewed and a link to their profile. (If you come up with the initial list of books, a VA/PA can be a great help when it comes to building the list of reviewers and tracking down all of their information to save you another task.)

There are also a whole range of book review sites where you can submit your book, some of which will republish their review on Amazon. For those that don't, you can republish the review yourself as an editorial review through your Amazon Author Central account as mentioned previously.

The submission process can vary depending on the individual site: some are paid while others are completely free; some require physical copies while others are happy with a PDF or Word document; some guarantee listings while with others you just send off your book and hope for the best.

1. Online submissions

Make a list of review sites: There are a lot of these sites on Google, so vet them based on the types of books they review (do they cover books like yours?) and the size of their audience.

As most review sites require a standard suite of information, gather yours and have all this ready to go. You can then easily submit to a range of sites in a single sitting (or ask your VA/PA to take care of it for you). This information normally includes:

- Book title, subtitle, author name and book price (eBook, paperback, hardback etc)
- Your professional author bio and headshot
- Book description
- Links to your book's listing on Amazon and/or other retailers
- An image of your book's cover
- Keywords (genre and other relevant terms)

Once you have made a note of all the information, gather it into a Word or Excel document so you simply copy and paste the information into your submission forms.

2. Paperback submissions

Unlike online submissions, where you'll likely receive a confirmation by email and alerted when your review is live, paperback submissions are much harder to track – it's unlikely you will be informed when your book arrives and if or when it gets reviewed. However, the only cost to you is a copy of your book and the cost of postage, so why not?

The steps are:

Compile a list of reviewers and review sites.

Write a covering letter to send with your book containing

the standard suite of information, which they will list on their website.

I appreciate how daunting this may feel, but building up a good number of reviews will help you to reach a whole new audience organically via Amazon as well as giving you so many exciting updates to share with your warmer audience.

8

BEYOND THESE PAGES

YOU HAVE OPTIONS

*T*he route you choose to publish will determine how much your hand is held along the way. The notion of this section is to give you an insight into what it would feel like to become an author with us.

We see you

Does that scare you or excite you? I have spent my entire career somewhere in between desperately wanting to be visible and fearful of getting noticed. Call it a mixture of passionately wanting to have a more significant impact in the world, mixed with a big dollop of imposter syndrome.

Who was I to be forging my own path in the vast world of publishing? I remember when I was first starting out, and I popped over an email to one of my biggest publishing inspirations, I was looking for that gentle hand on my back to encourage me to go for my dreams. The reply shocked me a little…

"What makes you think you are expert enough, and how do you even know if you are capable?"

I wasn't sure if she was being helpful or condescending, but it did make me look back over my life and experiences, which highlighted precisely why this was my moment to show the world my expertise.

Have you ever second-guessed yourself? Like my inspiration made me second-guessed myself? It's likely that at some point while deciding whether or not to write a book, you have told yourself one, if not all, of the following:

"No one will want to read what you write."

"Your ideas are bland, boring."

"Your ideas are too controversial."

"You'll never make enough money."

"You'll be laughed at."

"No publisher will accept it."

On and on.

Recognise any of those?

But that little voice doesn't have to stop you from writing your book, like it didn't stop me from writing mine. Do you want to know how you can drown it out? By not isolating yourself during the process.

When you attempt to write your book on your own, you only have your voice to listen to. When you decide to get support on the journey, you have our voices to listen to as well. Expert, caring and encouraging voices.

We hear you

Yes, above all that noise from others within your industry, we hear your voice. I know it can seem like you are sharing your message and not being listened to, but that isn't the case at all.

Your audience is merely waiting for you to showcase your knowledge with a little more authority. Anyone can write a post on social media, but only a true and knowledgeable expert can write a book on their subject matter.

Can I tell you the most prominent difference it made for me? It took me from feeling like I needed that validation from more experienced publishers to hearing these exact words from my clients: "I can't believe I'm writing my book with the industry leader." I mean… seriously.

Maybe it's your story that you want to be heard? After all, your life experiences can help you teach, empower and inspire others. Your story is important, it is of great value, and it will be your legacy.

We choose you

This is the bit that either scares the hell out of you or fills you with emotions of pure joy.

You don't need to make a submission and hope and pray for acceptance; we accept you, exactly as you are. You always were and always will be good enough.

Partnership publishing is a choice that YOU get to make; it's not a gamble or wish, it's a decision that you can make to share your voice, your message and your words with the world.

We just give a little more power to those words, together.

WHAT WE BELIEVE

*T*hat our authors must want to make a difference as well as making more money. Ultimately we believe that books must deliver readers change, transformation, healing, knowledge or power.

That an investment in yourself is an energetic exchange with the universe that says "I'm Ready." When we pay, we pay attention, and when we pay attention, we get better results.

As we serve you, you serve readers. Authors do not know best: become obsessed with what your readers want.

That no author should ever be left behind. Life sometimes gets in the way which is why traditional publishing deadlines can destroy dreams. Our work does not end until your book is out into the world making a difference, no matter what.

That there has to be a more even trade of value between traditional publisher and author, than the current model of taking 90% of the revenue. It isn't needed or necessary.

WHO WE WORK WITH

*W*e specialise in working with aspiring authors, professionals and entrepreneurs who are ready to stand out from the crowd and showcase their brilliance in a bestselling book.

Publishing your message in the form of a book truly invites opportunities like never before, with ease.

We can offer media, PR, radio and speaking opportunities to name a few! What could that do for your visibility?

Authors & Co take a proven and unique approach to positioning amazing individuals just like you for the success and clients that you deserve.

Why use all of that content for just social media and blog posts when becoming published is so much more powerful?

COLLABORATIVE PROJECTS

hen a chapter is enough...

Writing a solo book can feel daunting. The thought of writing 40,000 words just feels a step too far for some. That said, everyone has value to offer and a story to share. Sometimes a chapter is just enough.

Collaboration books are projects brought together with 10-20 women each adding value to the book. Each author contributes a chapter and has a taste of the bestseller experience.

Projects come about in two ways. Authors can bring their own concepts to Authors & Co or alternatively, as a company, we also bring our own book ideas to life and invite aspiring authors to join us.

KIND WORDS

"You would be daft NOT to work with Authors & Co. I have worked with Abigail and the team at Authors and Co to create my micro book "Closed Mouths Don't Get Fed". The book has created so many opportunities for me and has generated over six times my investment in sales and client centred conversions in the first month. I am SO excited to be writing and releasing a more formal and full book with Abigail and her team later this year. Abi's business ethic and her client centred values drew me to her company. The way she delivers for her clients is phenomenal. I can't recommend highly enough"

— DANI WALLACE – CELEBRITY SPEAKER COACH

"Writing and publishing a book with Authors & Co has been one of the best decisions I've ever made. The whole process from start to finish was amazing, I felt completely looked after by the whole team and nothing was ever too much trouble. Within a week of my book being published I was welcoming new clients directly from the book and had already made my investment back. Worth every single penny and more. If you work with Authors & Co you really won't regret it"

— JANE BAKER – HIGH END SALES COACH

"What an amazing experience from beginning to end with Abigail and the whole team at Authors & Co. I'd wanted to write a book for some time, but didn't have a clue how to go about taking my concept into a professional product that would sell. And then I met Abigail at an event, and the rest has happened in the blink of an eye! Abigail provides an exceptional and very personal service, adapting what she offers to meet your needs. Every step of the way she was there for me, promptly answering questions, offering advice and guiding me through the process. We worked to a clear plan, always keeping each other updated, and the whole project was a seamless and enjoyable experience. If we needed to shift the plan, Abigail and her team were extremely responsive and flexible. I never considered that writing a book would bring so many benefits to me personally and to my business. And the way Abigail goes about supporting you is a big part of that. A truly caring, authentic and professional outfit. Thank you so much for your partnership in bringing my book to life, I'm truly grateful. 'Have It All Without Burning Out' is down as one of my proudest moments :) I wouldn't hesitate to recommend Authors & Co to anyone wanting to release a book."

— DEBORAH BULCOCK - NUTRITIONAL
THERAPIST AND CONSULTANT

"Even though we are countries apart, Authors & Co made the entire process of writing much less stressful. They were quick to respond and help out in any way they could from that start of the project to the very final book print! I would highly recommend using this company."

— JULIE LADD – TELEHEALTH THERAPIST

"I have nearly tripled my income, been able to outsource more and work from home. I have a work/life balance at last."

— VANESSA DOOLEY - EARLY YEARS CONSULTANT

"I booked in 12 calls the week of the launch and I'm still getting calls scheduled in. I've landed more speaking gigs and since the book (1 month ago) I've made $30k in sales."

— ELAINE LOU CARTAS - BUSINESS COACH

"Working with Authors & Co has been amazing. The support has been second to none. The expert advice, knowledge and guidance has made the whole experience enjoyable, fun and life changing."

— CHELLE SHOHET - STYLIST

"I feel so grateful that I got to work with the incredible team at Authors & Co. They made everything so easy and the whole process has been an utter joy. Abi and her team are so honest and authentic, they definitely bring out the best in your writing."

— LORNA PARK - FOUNDER, MY GREAT BIG POSITIVE LIFE JOURNAL

"Their package is stupendous. It enables you to step up and into a whole new level for your business and personal journey. I am thoroughly pleased with my decision to go ahead with the team and feel like I have added so much value to what I do."

— KATE HENNESSEY BOWERS - HEALTH COACH

"Working alongside Authors & Co has made the process of being involved in a book collaboration not only exciting, but very professional too! I was supported and guided throughout, and no question was too small. The process was streamlined, and I can't recommend the company highly enough. Not to mention we achieved number 1 best seller on Amazon within 24 hours of it being launched! Thank you for everything!"

— CAROL-ANN REID – LIFE COACH

Please head to www.authorsandco.pub *to read many more...*

In 2017, Abigail Horne received the results from her genetic counselling session. As the practitioner turned the screen towards her, she saw a red cross and the word 'deceased' next to the name of her beloved grandad – Edward Hand. Abigail couldn't believe what she was seeing. All the memories of the man she adored, and they came down to just a small, red cross. She'd begged him to write his memories in a book she'd bought him when he was still alive, but it had remained untouched in a drawer. To this day, those blank pages still haunt her.

But far from it being his legacy, the red cross on the computer screen spurred Abigail into action. She began learning as much as she could about publishing and writing books so she could tell his story. It wasn't long before her company Authors & Co was born, and she'd written her own Amazon number one bestseller.

It's hard to believe this was the same person who just a year beforehand was hounded so much by online trolls that she was afraid to leave her house for twelve months.

Despite this, at the heart of everything for Abigail is a fierce desire to have a balance between business and being a mum. What matters most is being able to be there for her family, especially eight-year-old Ted, who is named in memory of her grandad.

And although he has been gone for ten years, Edward Hand is very much still part of their lives. Whenever Abigail needs strength, she thinks about what he would have done, and the love and shared memories.

It's something that also helps her cope with the crippling degenerative arthritis of her spine, which means she struggles to even pick her children up.

Abigail is a firm believer that everyone has a story and hurdles to overcome and through sharing these – you can help impact the lives of others. And whilst she has helped numerous entrepreneurs become best-selling authors, it's the legacy of their stories that matters the most. It's about ensuring that everyone remembers a life lived and cherished and not just a red cross on a computer screen.

So with nothing but love in Abigail's heart, Authors & Co was born, bridging the gap beautifully between traditional publishing and self-publishing.

Both options offered authors such value, yet neither offered a perfect solution. Abigail has a wonderful "nothing is too much trouble" style, offering authors all of the incredible professionalism and support of Traditional Publishing whilst retaining all of the royalties, rights and creative control of Self-Publishing.

Sourcing industry experts in different areas of the process, Abigail has developed a team of exceptional individuals to create a seamless and strategic author experience.

From concept and creation all the way through to the celebration of your launch and media features, Abigail has it all covered with her award-winning company.

A woman with a vision

Abigail Horne – Founder

Award Winning Entrepreneur & Founder of Authors & Co.

Abigail has worked with more than 10,000 individuals to help them fulfil their potential within corporate organisations and self-employed ventures.

No stranger to the media, Abigail has featured in Forbes as one of 21 women around the world to watch, The Huffington Post, Fox, Marie Claire and NBC as well as countless other media publications.

STAY IN TOUCH

Your story starts here...

If you're interested in finding out how we can work together to create your book, we'd love to share with you all the finer details of the author experience that we have created with skill and love.

Visit - www.authorsandco.pub

Email - hello@authorsandco.com

Follow us on Social Media - @authorsandco